Eugene, Oregon

a guide

by Mike Helm

Mike Helm

Illustrated by Brad Koekkoek

Rainy Day Press
PO Box 3035
Eugene, Oregon 97403

First Edition
Written and Published in 1979

Library of Congress Catalog Card Number
79-63656

International Standard Book Number
0-931742-01-3

Published by Rainy Day Press
PO Box 3035
Eugene, Oregon 97403

Edited by Jerry Keuter and Gene Ashby
Illustrated by Brad Koekkoek
Maps drawn by Christine Helm
Proofread by Patty Foster

For . . .

For Henry David Thoreau,
who showed me the ratrace,

and

For Christine, who didn't stop
cheering when I stopped running.

Contents

𑀕𑀕𑀕𑀕𑀕𑀕𑀕𑀕𑀕𑀕𑀕𑀕𑀕𑀕𑀕𑀕𑀕𑀕𑀕𑀕𑀕𑀕𑀕

Eugene:
A
Historical
Sketch

"Our little town has from 900 to
1000 inhabitants, One Episcopal
Church, One Old School Presbyterian
One...and one Methodist Meeting
House, 8 stores, 2 drug stores, two
hotel two Saloons, two printing offices, three Black, one tin & sheet
iron factory, one Goldsmith, 3
Waggon Shops, two Livery Stables One
market, one Shoe Shop, two Saddle &
Hemp makers one Saddle tree maker,
One grist & One Saw mill...One door
and Sash factory two Cabint Shops,
and one Post Office and your humble
servant has been for the last ten
years Post Master."

    Eugene F. Skinner
    to his sister,
    March 18, 1860

Significant Dates
in the History of Eugene

1812. The first white explorers, fur traders led by Donald McKenzie, reached the upper Willamette Valley.

1846. Lane County's first permanent settlers arrived. Eugene Skinner, William Dodson, Elijah Bristow, and Felix Scott crossed the plains in 1845, wintered in California, then headed north. All but Skinner claimed land in the Pleasant Hill area. Skinner marked his claim on the butte in the center of Eugene that now bears his name.

1847. More settlers arrived in the valley, including Charnel Mulligan, whose land claim adjoined Eugene Skinner's.

1848. The Territory of Oregon, extending from the summit of the Rocky Mountains to the Pacific Ocean, was created by the U. S. Congress. The first white child born in Lane County, a girl, was born to Mary Skinner.

1850. The Donation Land Law was passed by Congress, entitling settlers to free land in the west.
Lane County's population continued to climb.
Eugene Skinner became the first postmaster of the community called Skinner's

1851. The Territorial Legislature passed "An act to create and organize Lane County". Lane County was named for Joseph Lane, the first Territorial governor. Skinner's was surveyed and platted on a swampy site that soon became known as Skinner's

3

Mudhole, bounded by Water, Pearl, and 8th Streets, and an alley beyond Ferry Street.

1853. An election to choose a county seat from among four free land sites failed to win a majority. The county commissioners then chose 40 acres donated by Eugene Skinner and 40 adjoining acres donated by Charnel Mulligan. Thus Mulligan and Skinner became the co-founders of Eugene. Four blocks were retained for use as a public square and the rest was sold. The town was resurveyed and replatted on a higher site, out of the Mudhole. The name of the community, Skinner's, was changed to Eugene City. The County Clerk's office, a 16' x 20' building that now sits behind the Lane County Pioneer Museum, was built, "fronting on the public square".

1855. The first stage coaches began serving Eugene City, once each week over the West Territorial Road, and between Corvallis and Eugene via Winchester. The first courthouse was built at 8th and Oak Streets. It cost $8500 and was later moved one block north where it became the first Eugene High School.

1856. A big year for education. Eugene's first public school was built at the corner of what is now University and 25th Streets. A plaque at the site—now the Masonic Cemetery—says that the school was taught by Miss Sarah Ann Moore, who came daily from Goshen by horseback. The Cumberland Presbyterian Church established Columbia College on the lower part of what is now known as College Hill. The James Clinton, a steamboat, navigated the Willamette to Eugene City, establishing an expensive freight transport link with Portland.

1858. The first jail was built in Eugene City for $6500.

1859. Oregon became a state on February 14, and a Lane County man, John Whiteaker, became Oregon's first governor. He is buried in Eugene's Masonic Cemetery.

1862. Eugene City was incorporated.

1864. Telegraph wires reached Lorane.

1867. The first edition of the Eugene Guard was published.

1870. The population of Eugene City was 861.

1871. The Oregon and California Railway reached Eugene from Portland.

1874. A bridge was built to connect Eugene and Springfield.

1876. The first Ferry Street Bridge, a covered bridge, was built across the Willamette. The first students enrolled in the University of Oregon. John Wesley Johnson was the first president of the University and the school had four faculty members.

1887. The Eugene Electric Company, a private firm with a 100-horsepower generating plant, was granted a franchise by the city council for the city's first electric lighting system.

1888. Eugene City was renamed Eugene.

1891. Mule-powered street cars began operating in Eugene. "Except in case of emergency" the city council imposed a six mile per hour speed limit.

<u>1894</u>. Telephone service began in Eugene.

<u>1899</u>. The new courthouse was dedicated. A three-story brick building, it cost $50,000.

<u>1906</u>. There were four automobiles in Eugene.

<u>1911</u>. The Eugene Water and Electric Board was organized.

<u>1919</u>. Eugene Municipal Airport was established.

<u>1920</u>. Eugene's population was 10,593.

<u>1926</u>. American Express retired its last horses in Eugene.

<u>1927</u>. Streetcars stopped running in Eugene. KORE, Lane County's first commercial radio station, began broadcasting.

<u>1940</u>. 20,838 people lived in Eugene.

<u>1948</u>. The County began to allow zoning and to require building permits.

<u>1950</u>. Eugene's population was 35,879.

<u>1950's</u>. Much of old Eugene was demolished. The Osburn Hotel, the City Hall, the 1899 Courthouse, the old Post Office, and the Public Market were all torn down.

<u>1959</u>. A new Lane County Courthouse was built for $2 million.

<u>1960</u>. Eugene's population was 50,977.

<u>1962</u>. Eugene's new city hall was built.

<u>1966</u>. The population of Eugene rose to 75,300.

<u>1969-71</u>. Willamette Street was torn up and converted to the downtown mall.

<u>1973</u>. Eugene's population increased to more than 90,000.

<u>1975</u>. The Federal Building, U. S. Courthouse, was completed.

<u>1978</u>. The population of Eugene was 100,000.

<u>1979</u>. 103,500 people live in Eugene.

Meet
Eugene Skinner

Eugene F. Skinner, the founder of Eugene, Oregon, wrote the following letter to his sister, Phebe, who was living in what is now British Columbia.

Though most people who have lived in Eugene for any time know that their city was founded by Eugene F. Skinner and that he built a cabin on the north side of Skinner's Butte, he remains a fairly obscure figure to most of us. This letter will give you an idea of Skinner, the man, and his town in 1860.

March 18, 1860

My Dear Sister

        Yesterday evenings mail brot a long and wel-
come letter from you of date of Jany 20th 1860...
        It is now some 12 years since I have had
the pleasure of getting a letter from you direct,
before the one last evening...you are a Stranger
to this far off west and those that inhabit it,
and the beautiful scenes which surround us in
Oregon but could you but see our land of enchantment -- & we could be once more together in this
Country, we would try to live our childhood days
over again and I still hope to see you and our
brother in this country yet: the trip is not a
long one nor very expensive, and then I think that
was you and your kind companion in this Country
you could make a good living.
        Though the Country is new, we have no
aristocracy and no high style of living. Still
we enjoy life as well as those who roll in luxuries.
        My Dear Wifes health for a few years pased
has not been of the best, but she has pased that
critical period in woman and she is now...well
and becoming Stout and hearty. She is 46 years
old...
        As for our children they no nothing of
Sickness. They are verry larger of their ages.
Mary is as tall as I am & will outweigh me. The
next Leanora is more slender. Phebe is robust
and is as much like the original in our younger
days. St. John is said to by all to be as Smart
as the Smartest. Amilia soon will be five years
old & I think the Smartest of them all.

        The four older are going to School, as this
place there is a Cumberland Presbyterian College,
a primmarie School, and a high school. The high
school building is on my claim a little over ¼

8

mile from our house, the professor is an excellent
man a Graduate from Dublin College. I made the
arrangement for him to teach for 5 years from first
of December last, and am in hopes that my children will by that time have acquired a good education. Mary, beside the usual English, is
studying French. I intend to have her as well the
ballance to thuraly understand Mathematics. She
as well as St. John are quite good in figures.
Leanora is more dull, Phebe wont work. Spends
her time in reading.

Our school has about 50 students many of
them young women an...from 18 to 25 years. The
District school ¼ mile from our house has some
60 to 80 children mostly small. The College
1½ miles from our house has some 80 to 100 students.

Our little town has from 900 to 1000
inhabitants, One Episcopal Church, One Old School
Presbyterian one...and one Methodist Meeting
House, 8 stores, 2 drug stores, two Hotel two
Saloons, two Printing Offices, three Black, one tin
& sheet Iron factory, one Goldsmith, 3 Waggon
Shops, two Livery Stables One market, one Shoe
Shop, two Saddle & Hemp makers one Saddle tree
maker, One Grist & One Saw mill...One door and
Sash factory two Cabint Shops, and one Post Office
and your humble servant has been for the last ten
years Post Master.

In the month of november last we had a full
of some 2 inches of snow one night--the next morning it looked Irregular to see Tomato Pumpkin
Cucumbers & Bean blossoms Peering through the Snow
it was all gone by ten o'clock and the vine Continued to blossom until about the middle of Dec....
Ice formed on the ponds...none in the stream, to
the thickness of 3 inches which the boys used for
skating....my Peach & Almond trees are in full
bloom StrawburyBloom have been seen every month
this winter....

9

Stock require little or no feed in Oregon in winter unless near a town. I have some 100 h of cows & stock cattle and they have no feed this winter except what nature provides, upon the whole will candidly say that was I offered all--and be compelled to live there or live oregon on a bare subsistance I would take Oregon as it is nothing more than a bare subsistance that we have in any country, tis not wealth, but Contentment and a Conscience clear of offence that makes the sum total of this life.

I am tolerable well off in property. Suppose my property is worth farr from all uncumberence about $2000.00 probably I owne $300.00. I have an expensive family but a very equnomical wife. I buy everything that I eat & ____ dont farm any not able have the asthma very bad at times getting old, wont expect to Stay long in world and when I leave would like to have a clean balanced sheet for wife and children.

Eugene F. Skinner

Bicycle History Tours

Though Eugene streets are clearly divided between east and west at Willamette Street, the preponderance of historically significant sites in east Eugene made it necessary for me to include sites nominally in east Eugene in the tour I've called the Bicycle History Tour of West

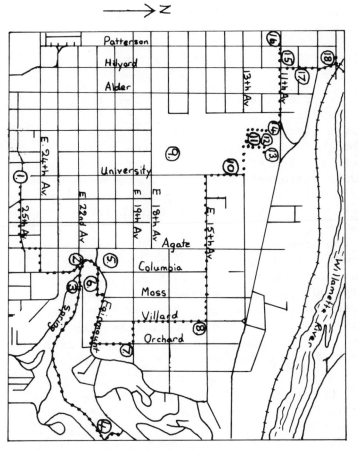

East Eugene Bicycle History Tour

Eugene.

These exact routes were designed with the bicycle in mind, but the tours may also be easily accomplished, with slight deviations from the prescribed routes, by people in automobiles.

●●●

A Bicycle History Tour
of East Eugene

Our east Eugene history tour begins at 25th and University Streets, the Masonic Cemetery (1), where a plaque marks the site of Eugene's first school. This old cemetery is the burial site of Eugene F. Skinner, the founder of Eugene, and of John Whiteaker, Oregon's first governor. (For a more complete description of the Masonic Cemetery, see "Eugene's Old Cemeteries", this chapter.)

From here move east, along 25th Street, to your left as you face up the hill into the cemetery. For one block 25th is an unpaved alley, but the pavement resumes at the Onyx Street end of the alley. Stay on 25th Street until you get to Agate Street, then turn left. Go one block along Agate to the 24th Street intersection, where you will turn right.

One block along 24th will find you at the Columbia Street intersection. Turn left here and keep thinking "up", though Columbia at first appears to go down. After a couple of blocks, there is a 'Y'. Only bicycles may continue up the hill to the right, and that is the route we will follow.

The old train tracks (2) embedded in the concrete along this part of Columbia Street mark the route once travelled by streetcars. Streetcar service was established in Eugene in 1891 and

came to an end in 1927. We will see more of
these tracks later in our tour as we move along
Fairmount Boulevard.

At the intersection of Columbia and Fairmount, take a hard right, uphill again along
Fairmount Boulevard.

You are now in an area of extremely gracious
older homes. Treetops (3), at the intersection
of Fairmount and Spring Boulevards, is perhaps the
largest and most gracious of them all. This stately
old house sits high on a knoll far from the
street, surrounded by a park-like area of mature
oak trees. The house and grounds were a gift,
in 1938, to the University of Oregon, made by
the Church family, at that time headed by Campbell
Church, stepson of Prince Lucien Campbell. Prince
Lucien Campbell was the fourth president of the
University of Oregon.

Treetops is the home of the Chancellor of
the State System of Higher Education, Roy Lieuallen.
A clause in the agreement between the University and
the Church family states that the house must be
used as the home of the Chancellor or the President
of the University or ownership of the house will
revert to the Church family.

Follow Fairmount to your left. As you
travel along the side of this little urban mountain you will be treated to a panoramic view of
Eugene. On the fourth of July this is a favorite
viewpoint of people who come to watch the fire-
works display in Autzen Stadium, easily visible
from here.

The road into Hendricks Park (4) will take
you through a small, wild forest, and then into
the park itself. Most of the land for Hendricks
Park was given to the City of Eugene in 1906
by Thomas G. and Martha A. Hendricks.

It's all downhill from here. Turn around
and follow Fairmount Boulevard back the way you
came, through the forest, past Treetops, on round
to Washburne Park (5) at the intersection of 21st
and Fairmount. Stop here and look through the
bushes at the park and wading pool, once the
front lawn for the Washburne family who lived in
the large white house (2425 Fairmount Boulevard)
overlooking the park from directly behind you.
The park was given to the city in 1958 in memory
of Minnie L. Washburne.

Turn right on McMorran Street and follow
it around until it once again joins Fairmount
Boulevard. As you go along McMorran, notice the
large English tudor house above the wall on
the right side of the street (2315 McMorran).
This house was partly given and partly sold to
the State by the McMorran family in 1941. Today
it is the home of the President of the University
of Oregon, William Boyd.

Turn right on Fairmount and ride through one
of Eugene's loveliest older neighborhoods. The
large houses with their expansive lawns are representative of residential development that took
place between 1920 and 1940.

Follow Fairmount Boulevard to Orchard
Street and turn left. The large white white house
on the southeast corner of 19th and Orchard (2020
E. 19th) is the oldest house in this area. The
original Orchard Street House (7) was built in
the 1870's.

Our next stop is the Maude Kerns Art Center
(8). Take 19th Street to your left for one block,
then turn right at Villard Street. On the southeast corner of 15th and Villard is the Maude
Kerns Art Center, once known as the Fairmount
Presbyterian Church. Completed in 1895, this is
the oldest church building in Eugene. An example
of the Georgian Revival Style of architecture,
the original building has been modified to house
gallery and workshop space for the art center.

The art center is named for Maude Kerns, a local artist who died in 1965.

Now we will enter the University of Oregon campus. Turn left from Villard onto 15th Street and follow 15th west to University Street. At the 15th and University Street intersection, look across the street to your left. That parklike area of large fir and cedar trees is the Pioneer Cemetery (9). (For a more complete history and description of the Pioneer Cemetery, see Eugene's Old Cemeteries, this chapter. For a description and history of some of the artwork you may pass on this swing through the campus, see the UO Art Walk in Chapter 2.) I recommend a stroll through the cemetery before continuing.

Now, down the hill and left at the intersection of 13th and University. The Collier House (10), the large yellow Victorian house on your left, was built in 1885 by George Collier, then a professor at the University. (For more on the Collier House, see Chapter 5.)

Down 13th Street, about 100 yards from the traffic barricades, the Pioneer Father, a dramatic bronze sculpture, strides out of the Old Quad. Take one of the paths through the Old Quad, behind the Pioneer Father. The two old buildings in the farthest left-hand corner of the quad are the original buildings on the University campus. The first is Deady Hall, the second is Villard Hall.

Deady Hall (11) is representative of the French Second Empire style of architecture. It has been incontinuous use since it opened in 1876, and, for the first ten years of its existence, it was the entire University. Deady Hall was guaranteed, at the time of its opening, for 1000 years, barring earthquakes. It was named, in 1893, for Judge Matthew P. Deady, a member of the Oregon Supreme Court Bench, and president of the University's first Board of Regents.

Villard Hall (12) is a more elaborate example of the French Second Empire architectural style. Villard opened in 1886 and is named after Henry

15

Villard, a financial leader in the Northwest who, during a financial crisis in 1881, assumed responsibility for the University's debts and prevented the sale of Deady Hall to the University's creditors.

Between Villard Hall and the bank that drops onto Franklin Boulevard, a short stone pillar (13) juts from the grass. This is a gift of the Class of 1893, a break with the tradition followed by previous classes of planting memorial trees. A plaque commemorating the Class of 1897 is visible on a massive oak tree near the wall. The tree immediately to its right has nearly swallowed a plaque commemorating the Class of 1900.

Many of the trees in this area were blown over during the Columbus Day Storm in 1962. At least one, a huge cedar tree, has been prudently topped to help prevent a repeat of that catastrophe.

Leave these old buildings via the concrete walkway that leads down the small hill from the back steps of Deady Hall. At the bottom of the hill, pause to look back at Deady and view the old building framed at the top of an avenue of fir trees.

Now turn to your right and leave the campus passing down the little road that leads between the Robinson Theatre and out through the Dads Gates (14). These iron gates, now suffering from flaking paint and an abundance of rust, once marked the main entrance to the campus. The gates were given by the Dads Club to the University in 1941.

Our objective now is to go west on East 11th Street. Be careful of the traffic as you turn to your left in front of the gates. Get as far into the right lane as you can and you'll soon find yourself travelling with the traffic in a bicycle lane, passing Northwest Christian College.

A half block beyond Northwest Christian

Calkins House (1902)

College, at 751 East 11th, is the <u>Patterson</u> <u>House</u>
(15), more famous recently as the Animal House.
This house was built by Dr. A. W. Patterson, an
early Eugene area physician and surveyor, who
finished it a year before his death in 1904. It
has been, in addition to a stylish family residence, a fraternity house and, presently, a work-
release center for men who are on work-release
from state correctional facilities. This is
also where the film <u>Animal</u> <u>House</u> was made in
1977.

Continue on 11th Street for one more block,
to the intersection of 11th and Patterson. There,
on the southwest corner, is the <u>Calkins</u> <u>House</u>
(16). This Queen Anne style house was built in
1902 by W. W. Calkins, a successful Eugene
banker, when this area was the fashionable area
of Eugene.

Now, double back on the sidewalk, so that you
won't end this tour as an ornament on someone's
pick-up, to the intersection of Hilyard and 11th.
There, follow the bicycle lane north, toward
Franklin Boulevard.

About half a block from the Hilyard Street
intersection with 11th Street, a willow-hung millrace flows through fraternity house backyards and
under Hilyard Street. The millrace (17) was
completed in 1852 when Hilyard Shaw and a partner, Avery Smith, excavated a ditch to connect
two old sloughs on Shaw's land claim. The millrace started at Judkins Point and ended where
the Ferry Street Bridge now stands. A sawmill
and a gristmill were built by 1856 and the millrace became the industrial arterial of Eugene.

Cross Franklin Boulevard and stay on Hilyard
Street until it intersects with East 8th Street.
Turn left just before the railroad tracks. About
100 yards down 8th Street are the Jorgensen
Apartments. The final stop on our tour is
the building that appears to be an old barn,
just behind the Jorgensen Apartments.

This old barn was once known as <u>Abram's</u>
<u>Cider</u> <u>and</u> <u>Vinegar</u> <u>Mill</u> (18). Now a shambling,
unpainted wreck, quietly acceding to the demands
of time and nature and neglect, it was once
capable of producing over fifty barrels of apple
cider and drying 150 bushels of plums in a
single day. Built in 1883, it is one of the
last remnants of boom times on the millrace.
        Our tour ends here, at this old barn.
From here you have easy access to the bike path
that runs along the south side of the Willamette.
Return to the railroad tracks near the intersection of 8th and Hilyard Streets, cross the
tracks and the EWEB property beyond, and you're
on the bike path.

* *

<u>A</u> <u>Bicycle</u> <u>History</u> <u>Tour</u>
<u>of</u> <u>West</u> <u>Eugene</u>

        We'll begin our historical tour of west
Eugene on the top of Skinner's Butte. From here,
if you look due south, right down Willamette
Street, you will see Eugene's other major landmark,
Spencer Butte.
        <u>Skinner's</u> <u>Butte</u> (1) was named for Eugene
F. Skinner, the founder of Eugene, as was the
park through which we will soon pass.
        No one knows for sure how <u>Spencer's</u> <u>Butte</u>
(2), that glowering hill seven miles south of
here, got its name, though there are several
popular theories. One is that it is named for
a Hudson's Bay Company trapper who wandered away
from the other members of his expedition and was
killed by Indians on the Butte. Another poss-

19

ibility is that it was named by Dr. Elijah White, the leader of an exploratory expedition in 1845, for John C. Spencer, who was then Secretary of War.

As you leave the top of Skinner's Butte, bear around to your right and you will soon be riding on the road that runs through Skinner's Butte Park. The Willamette will be on your left, the Butte on your right.

At the base of Skinner's Butte, where we are now, is where Eugene Skinner first settled in 1846. He intended to build a cabin on the river-bank, but was dissuaded from doing so by local Indians who warned him that the Willamette often overflowed its banks and flooded his intended building site. A replica of Skinner's tiny cabin (3) was placed on his approximate building site in 1970.

Keep going in this direction and you will leave the park on High Street, which will take you through the East Skinner Butte Neighborhood (4).

The East Skinner Butte Neighborhood developed as people who had originally built houses in downtown Eugene sought refuge from high pro-perty taxes, the inevitable result of rising city center land value. At this writing, some of the houses are receiving much-needed repair and re-novation. Others, however, are suffering from terminal neglect.

Four houses that are worth mentioning, though they are not all in good repair, are:

The Koppe House, a Queen Anne style house, was built in the 1890's, the residence of Emil Koppe, head of the Eugene Woolen Mill Company. It is located at 205 East 3rd Street.

The Miller House, at 246 East 3rd, was built in the 1870's by Eugene real estate developer George Melvin Miller. Miller was a versatile man who, in addition to laying out the Fairmount area of Eugene and facilitating the establish-ment of the town of Florence, once invented a flying machine.

20

West Eugene Bicycle History Tour

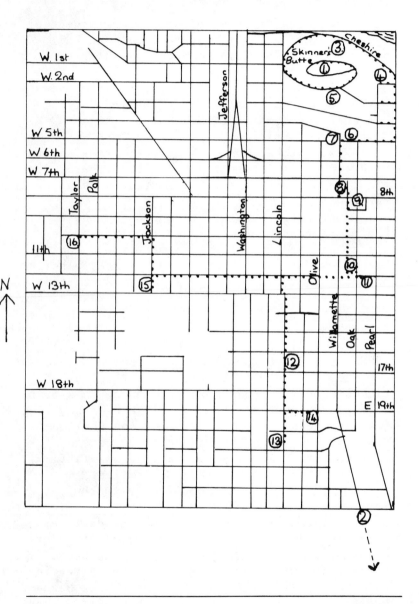

The Henderson House, at 260 High Street, ori-
ginally stood downtown. It is an example of the
Classic Greek Revival style of architecture.
Built in the 1850's, it was once the home of
Reverend Enoch Pinckney Henderson, President of
Columbia College from 1856 to 1859. We will
visit the site of Columbia College later in
this tour.

The Watts House, at 335 Pearl, is a Queen Anne
Style house that was built in the 1890's. It
was once the home of J. O. Watts, a Eugene
jeweler and optician.

Now, get back on High Street, cross the railroad tracks, and turn right at 5th Street. Continue on 5th Street to Willamette, where you will
turn left.

Just before you get to Andy's Eugene Station,
the restaurant on the northeast corner of the
Willamette and 5th Street intersection, look
back toward Skinner's Butte, now directly north
of you. That elaborate green Queen Anne Style
house peering at the town from the forest at the
base of Skinner's Butte is the Shelton-McMurphey
House.

The Shelton-McMurphey House (5) was built in
1888 for $7000 by Dr. T. W. Shelton, a Eugene
physician. Pictures of the house taken at the
time of construction show it standing on a nearly
treeless Skinner's Butte, overlooking a bustling
frontier town. A better view of the Shelton-
McMurphey house can be had from the platform of
the Southern Pacific Railroad Station platform,
one block behind Andy's Eugene Station.

Andy's Eugene Station, the restaurant at 27
East 5th Street, is housed in the Oregon Electric
Railway Depot building (6). The building was
built in 1914 in the Georgian Revival Style of
architecture. The Oregon Electric was Oregon's
longest inter-urban electric railway, extending
all the way from Portland to Eugene. It began
operations in Eugene in 1912. The building has

22

Shelton-McMurphey House (1888)

been beautifully restored inside and deserves a visit, even if you don't intend to eat.

Across Willamette Street from the Oregon Electric Depot building, at 488 Willamette Street, is the Palace Hotel (7). The Palace fell on hard times during the 1920's, but prior to that it was a fashionable and popular hotel, conveniently located near the Oregon Electric Depot, the Southern Pacific Depot, and the terminus of Eugene's street-car line. The Palace was built in 1903 and currently houses offices and small retail shops.

Now, turn south, or left, on Willamette, toward Spencer's Butte which you can see standing above the town as you look up Willamette Street. Two and a half blocks from here, on the left side of Willamette, is another of Eugene's early hotels, the Smeede.

The Smeede Hotel (8), 767 Willamette, was built in 1885 and was known then as Baker's Hotel, "...the finest hotel building between Salem and Red Bluff, California...", a home in Eugene for influential and wealthy travellers. Though many changes have taken place both in and around the Smeede, the hotel's original name can still be seen in bronze letters embedded in the sidewalk in front of the building.

Take the alley that runs along the north, or left, side of the Smeede Hotel, turn right at the end and proceed across West 8th Street on West Park Street. The little inner-city park on your left is known as the Park Blocks (9).

Once known as Hitching Post Square, the Park Blocks are the result of a directive in the original land grant to the city by Charnel Mulligan. Mulligan and Eugene Skinner each donated 40 acres from their respective land claims for the building of a town. Mulligan directed that four acres be set aside for a new courthouse. The square soon became a center for public gatherings. (For more on the Park Block sculptures and fountains, see "A Downtown Art Walk", in Chapter 2.)

Leave the Park Blocks via the southwest corner
and cut through the Merrill Lynch parking lot to
the downtown mall, where you must walk your bike.
There is a walkway between Olson's Jeweler's
and the Broadway, directly in front of you.
Take it. At the end of the walkway, a wide,
paved alley stretches before you. Ride on.
Cross 10th Street and continue in the alley on the
other side. About midway in the block between
10th and 11th Streets, look up and slightly to
your left. The large silver dome looming over
the buildings facing 11th Street is the First
Christian Church (10), our next stop. You can
reach it via the alley, thus avoiding Eugene's
heavy city center traffic.

The First Christian Church was built in 1911,
at a cost of $90,000. In 1926 the tower, which
housed the first chimes in Eugene, was added.
On the Oak Street side of the church, near a
sign pointing the way to the administrative
offices, are two large locust trees. These were
planted in the 1860's and stood at the foot of
a long driveway leading to the Dunn house, an
early Eugene residence then located to the
west of the Church.

Cross Oak Street at the 12th Street cross-
walk. The last house facing 12th on the first
block, 170 E. 12th, is the Christian House (11),
built by Daniel Christian in 1855, one of the
oldest houses in Eugene. This house is representative of the Greek Revival style of architecture. The joists, sills, and flooring in
the old house are the original items. The
Christian House is the only original frame house
in Eugene built by a homesteader that still remains on its Donation Land Claim. Workmen strip-
ping the walls during a renovation in 1979 found
newspapers from the 1860's which had been used
as insulation.

Turn around and go west on 12th Street,
across Oak Street. Cut through the alley and

25

parking lot to Willamette Street, through the
alley by Eugene Hospital and Clinic, and then
keep going west on West 12th Street. Turn
left on Lincoln and go south to 1611, where the
Peters-Liston-Wintermeier House (12) is quietly
sagging into the ground.

The Peters-Liston-Wintermeier House was
built in 1869-1870 and is the only known Rural
Gothic Style house in Lane County. It may be the
finest example of that style, which features
verticality and irregularity of outline, in
the Willamette Valley. Some of the materials
used in the construction of this house were made
in France and came to Eugene via the Horn of
South America and San Francisco.

Keep going on Lincoln to 2056, the Lansdowne
House (13).

This lovely old Victorian house was purchased
by Frederick Smith, a Springfield farmer, in
1902 for $2000. The trim on the house is called
Victorian gingerbread and it could then be ordered
ready-made from catalogues.

Now, turn around and go back to 19th Street.
Turn right on 19th and go two blocks to Olive.
Stop.

This hill is known as College Hill. A plaque
set here, at the corner of 19th and Olive, tells
you why. Columbia College (14) whose name in
the history books is usually prefaced by the
adjective "ill-fated", opened on this site in
1856. It was established by the Cumberland
Presbyterian Church and, in its first year of
existence, has 52 students. The building burned
down twice before, in 1860, Columbia College
closed forever.

Go back to Lincoln Street, turn right to 12th
Street, then left to Jackson Street. On Jackson
Street turn left to 1268 Jackson, the former home
of geologist Thomas Condon.

The Condon House (15) was built on the south-

26

west corner of 11th and High Streets in 1878, and purchased by Mr. and Mrs. Condon in 1882. Condon originally came to Oregon in 1852, as a missionary for the Congregational Church. In that capacity he established a church in The Dalles, where he and his parishioners began collecting valuable geological data and specimens, some of which they sent to the Smithsonian Institution in Washington, D. C. When the University of Oregon opened in 1876 he became the first head of the Department of Natural Sciences.

Now, turn around and go north on Jackson to 10th Street. Turn left on 10th and keep going, clear to Taylor Street. The large Victorian house on the southwest corner of 10th and Taylor is the honeymoon cottage of Frank and Ida Hendricks Chambers.

The Chambers House (16) was built in 1891 by Frank Chambers, a Eugene hardware merchant, for his bride. The couple moved into the house immediately after their wedding and lived there until Ida's death in 1901. The house originally stood at the intersection of Broadway and Lincoln Streets. The Victorian gingerbread on the house was not ordered from a catalogue, but made to order at Midgeley's Planing Mill on the millrace.

Our tour ends here, at this honeymoon cottage. Go on about your business with a little of the romance of early Eugene in your heart and a little more knowledge of your city in your head.

Eugene's
Old Cemeteries

Most of Eugene's old
cemeteries are islands of
virgin forest in an ever-
expanding sea of hectic urban humanity, handy refuges
where one can withdraw easily for an hour or so of
quiet contemplation and
solitude, or for an imaginary trip back into history.
If, some warm day soon,
you are looking for a
quiet place, perhaps for
lunch in a place more con-
ducive to thought than the
vinyl booths at MacDonald's,
try brown-bagging to an old
cemetery.

The
Masonic Cemetery

University and 25th Streets

It is unfortunate that Eugene's most historic
cemetery is also its most vandalized and least
cared for cemetery. It rises abruptly on a hill-
side from the flatness south of the University.
A plaque near the street says that this was the
site of Eugene's first school, built in the
1850's and taught by Miss Sarah Ann Moore, who
came daily to the school by horseback from
Goshen. The cemetery was platted in 1859.

Tall firs and high brush offer a sharp
contrast to the neatly-kept lawns of the small
frame houses lining the streets that border the
lower end of the cemetery. Once past this, the
peacefulness of the little forest and the historical significance of the place take over.
The names of Eugene's streets, parks, and
schools leap at us from the tombstones.

John Whiteaker, Oregon's first governor,
and captain of a wagon train to Oregon in 1852,
lies here with seven members of his family.
They are all together in a ghastly quonset hut
mausoleum, slipped in there like loaves of
bread into a concrete oven.

"Eugene F. Skinner, Born in Essex, New York,
September 13, 1809, Founded Eugene City June 5,
1853, Died at Eugene City, December 15, 1864",
reads an old concrete slab-type tombstone. Near
him lies "Marguerite Skinner Smith, Granddaughter
of Eugene F. Skinner, 1882-1960". Surely she was
something else to someone else in her 78 years.

Maude Kerns (Maude Kerns Art Center), T. G.
Hendricks (Hendricks Park), J. B. Chambers
(Chambers Street), Ida Patterson (Patterson Ele-

30

mentary School), Andrew Wilson Patterson (Patterson Street), M. Luther Dillard (Dillard Road),
Mahlon and Elizabeth Harlow (Harlow Road),
Francis Berrian Dunn (Dunn Elementary School),
and John Wesley Johnson, the first president of
the University of Oregon, are all buried here.

Stand on top of the hill and think of
Eugene City on the day in 1864 when Eugene
Skinner was buried here. The forest stretched
all the way to the river. A Eugene City of 100,000
people and nearly that many automobiles was beyond
the wildest dreams of those who attended the burial.
Probably this little patch of wilderness is not
much changed from that day. It is peaceful here.
An impish wind rustles the trees, muffling the
exhaust pipe sounds of contemporary urban life.
The cemetery is a restful interlude in a busy
day.

* *

The Laurel Hill Cemetery

West Springfield

This was a quiet, forested hill-top in
1855 when William, the 5-year-old son of Zara
and Maria Sweet, was buried here at the base of
an already mature fir tree.

A hundred or so years later Interstate 5
sliced through the valley and the quiet of

Laurel Hill was lost to the sizzling and zinging of tires and the roar of engines hustling cargo north and south. Later, Farwest Steel and Sears opened warehouses at the base of the hill, adding their commercial clatter to the roar of I-5. Then the Oregon State Highway Department bulldozed a clearing right next to the cemetery where they now store old equipment, logs, and gravel, and where Highway Department employees cut firewood on Sundays. Next, Lane County built a solid waste transfer and recycling facility at the bottom of the hill. Last, the cemetery was logged. Today most of the big trees are only massive stumps.

The Laurel Hill Cemetery is a decimated island of tranquility, an unsuccessful refuge from the roar, hum, zip, and belch of traffic, commerce, and garbage. Though it is not an ideal spot for brown-bagging a quiet lunch hour, it is included here because the founders of two cities are buried here, and enough is left of old Oregon to stir the imagination.

Old graves include those of Isaac and Betsey Briggs, "Pioneers of 1847". Isaac Briggs is the founder of Springfield. Charnel Mulligan, founder with Eugene Skinner of Eugene, was buried here in 1899. Also buried here are several members of the Judkins family (Judkins Point), "Pioneers of 1852".

Picture in your mind a lady called Missouri Clearwater. She is buried here beside her husband, J. A. Was she tall, with dark hair and flashing eyes and a smile that just levelled old J. A.? Easier to imagine, if names can be a guide to character and appearance, is Hanover E. Pitts, buried here beside his wife, Violetta. Probably a banker, a Yale graduate, an aristocrat among the rude hicks of his time in Springfield.

If you wear earplugs and blur your vision a little, the Laurel Hill Cemetery is worth a visit.

32

Mt. Calvary Cemetery

300 Mary Lane

High on a hill just south of central Eugene is the Mt. Calvary Cemetery. From here the town seems to roll across the valley like a wave and splash against the purple and blue wall of the Coburg Hills to the north. Mt. Calvary, a Catholic cemetery, is far enough from the roar of commerce that the sounds are muted, and the neatly-mown lawn and majestic firs provide the visitor with a restful, parklike place to spend a few moments in the middle of a busy day.

Names on the tombstones here read like an eastern European telephone book: Cersosfsky, Ziolkowski, Rodakowski, Hrynchuk, Kolker, Farquharson, Skvarek, Kunstatsky, Krupka, Splonskowski, Ziolkowski, Kowalski, Taubenkrau, Dombrowski, Karowski, Sprouffske.

Graves here date back to the 1890's. The major reason for visiting Mt. Calvary is not old graves but the restfulness of the setting. The view is spectacular and the grass soft.

Unfortunately, you must walk and sit carefully. Mt. Calvary's neighbors see it as just another huge green doggy playpen and latrine.

The Pioneer Cemetery

18th & University Streets

Directly across University Street from McArthur Court on the University of Oregon campus, a large stone Union Army sentry stands guard over 47 Civil War veterans and a few of their wives. They lie, neatly dressed and covered, in three precise ranks beneath concrete tombstones that bear the name of each soldier's army outfit. "37 Ill. Inf., 17 Wis. Inf., 1 Ore. Cav., 2 Wis. Cav., 2 Mass Cav., 49 N. Y. Inf., 14 N. Y. H. Art., 3 Mo. Cav...." They came from all over the United States to lie permanently in this peaceful grove of mature Douglas fir, redwood, holly, and cedar trees.

The Pioneer Cemetery, formerly the Odd Fellows' Cemetery, was platted in 1873, long before the University of Oregon grew to its present size and began to crowd it on three sides. Like any other old cemetery, this one stretches the visitor's mind back to earlier times.

White, mossy tombstones tell of

Ja. Goodchild
born
In Berks. County England
Dec. 4, 1813
Died
In Eugene City, Ogn.
Jan. 20, 1881

34

and

Johanna
Goodchild
Born in
Stockholm
Sweden
Dec. 3, 1823
Died
S. 24, 1882

Elizabeth Gulliford, "Native Daughter", was
buried here in 1932. Nine members of the Hulen
family are buried nearby, with 99 years separating
the burial dates of the first and last Hulen
interred in the family plot.

A visitor is more apt to encounter things
which seem bizarre in the Pioneer Cemetery than
in any of Eugene's other cemeteries. These are
nice touches, though, that make the visit a
little more memorable. For instance, in the late
afternoon, a bag-piper often marches among
the tombstones, playing music only the dead
could enjoy up close. Across the cemetery, the
music coming through the trees is lonely, haunting,
and melancholy. Other solitary musicians often
practice nestled against the trunk of a giant
Douglas fir or cedar tree. The soft strum of
guitar floats on the breeze in the company of
saxophone, flute, or other musical instrument.
Amorous couples snuggle in the lush grass in
the spring and summer, and a midnight runner
passing through the cemetery on Hallowe'en
hears eery laughter, too boisterous to be
otherworldly. On golden fall afternoons the
University Marching Band practices on an adjoining field and a cemetery visit can be
conducted to the sound of drums and brass and
the imagined cheers of a ghostly crowd.

One of the nicest walks in Eugene is through
the University campus and the Pioneer Cemetery.

The
Mulkey Cemetery

West of Hawkins Lane
South of Trillium

> Remember friends, as you pass by,
> As you are now, so once was I.
> As I am now, you soon will be.
> So prepare for death and follow me.
>> From the tombstone of
>> William and Matilda Montgomery
>> Buried in the Mulkey Cemetery
>> in 1910 and 1901

This small, old cemetery is strangled by modern, ranch style houses that have grown incongruously on its perimeter, and the once magnificent oak tree in its center appears barely to have survived an attack by a psychopathic tree surgeon. It is windswept, barren, and lonely on a cold winter morning, and it is hard to imagine that its character would soften on even the warmest summer day.

Gravestones in the Mulkey Cemetery date back to the 1850's, so even with its minimal aesthetic appeal, it deserves a visit from anyone who wants to stretch his or her imagination back to the days when the first white people settled in Eugene. Also, the Mulkey Cemetery has Eugene's best preserved examples of the quaint and plaintive verse characteristic of grave markers in older cemeteries. Consider the following.

Amiable, she won all.
Intelligent, she charmed all.
Fervent, she loved all.
Dead, she saddened all.
>   From the tombstone of
>   Magdalene, wife of R. Scott,
>   February 11, 1799-May 10, 1883

Life is not our own,
'Tis but a loan
To be repaid

The debt is due
The dream is o'er.
Life's but a shade.
>   From the tombstone of
>   Rosellia, wife of
>   James M. Nettleton,
>   June 29, 1850-June 9, 1903

Asleep in Jesus, blessed sleep,
From which none ever wake to weep.
A calm and undisturbed repose,
Unbroken by the lust of foes.
>   From the tombstone of
>   Hester A. Mulkey
>   September 20, 1825-September 1, 1888

Names of Eugene's streets and residential districts spring from the tombstones here, too--Barger, Conger, Blanton, Hawkins. 1862 was a hard year for the Mulkey family. Five Mulkeys were buried on this hilltop in that year, including two young children of W. H. and L. Mulkey.

For a brief glimpse into the lives and deaths of the pioneers of west Eugene, the Mulkey Cemetery is worth a visit.

...upon the whole will candidly say
that was I offered all--and be compared
to live there or live oregon on a bare
subsistance I would take Oregon as it
is nothing more than a bare subsistance
that we have in any country, tis not
wealth, but Contentment and a Conscience
clear of offence that makes the sum
total of this life.

> Eugene Skinner
> to his sister
> March 18, 1860

Cultural Eugene:

A Guide to the Finer Things in Oregon's Cultural Center

Beall Concert Hall

People in Eugene may have access to more books, concerts, theater performances, art classes, galleries, and museums than people in any other city of similar size in the United States.

The largest library in Oregon is in
Eugene. Musical concerts occur almost
nightly at the University of Oregon's
Beall Hall. Theater groups provide fine
dramatic performances year round. Locally
and nationally-acclaimed performers grace
the stage at the Community Center for the
Performing Arts. Rock concerts are held
at McArthur Court. Painting, sculpture,
and photography are on continual display
in Eugene's many galleries.

Culture has even worked its way into
the commercial center of the city, evi-
denced by the number of works in the downtown area (see "A Downtown Art Walk", this
chapter), and the plan, for the summer of
1979, to present a Shakespeare play
at the fountain on the downtown mall.

Eugene is a comfortable and encouraging home for artists, craftsmen, artisans,
and patrons of the arts.

Art
in Public Places

A University Art Walk

The most notable art collection in Eugene is
in the University of Oregon Museum of Art. The
University also serves as home to many works of
art located in easy public view outside the Museum.
If you are interested in art and have some time
to spare, come along with me on a University
art walk.

We begin our University art walk at Hayward
Field, at the north end of the west grandstand.
The Event (1), a large iron sculpture, depicts
a classic male athletic figure hurtling a
barrier. The Event was cast in 1976 by Ray
L. Edwards and donated to the University in
memory of Rupert J. Marks by his parents. The
flight of the cast figure is arrested at the top
of his leap, a young athlete symbolically frozen
in time, forever young, athletic, and competitive.

Now, leave Hayward Field via the northwest
gate, cross 15th Street and take the walkway
that leads between the dormitories and the tennis
courts, past Carson Hall to 13th Street. The
new brick building in front of you is Science
III.

In the lobby of Science III, a large bronze
gull swoops across an imaginary body of water,
dipping one wing-tip while the other stretches
for the sky. Nature and motion have been captured by the sculptor, Tom Hardy, in one of
the most dramatic modern pieces on the campus.
Completed in 1973, Touching a Wave (2) is ded-
icated to the memory of Paul L. Risley, a former
professor of biology, who died in 1971.

From here, walk west, up 13th Street. Just
past the old wood frame buildings on your right,
is the science complex.

At the edge of the lawn that lies between you
and the science complex is a sundial (3) mounted
in a block of granite. The sundial was the gift,
in 1912, of the parents of Wilson Mays, a 1909
graduate of the University who died in 1910,
in his memory. It is made of bronze and in-
scribed with Latin phrases lamenting the swift
passage of time.

Until the fall of 1978 a replica of the
15-ton Willamette meteorite stood in the courtyard of the science complex. It disappeared
one night, only to mysteriously reappear a few
nights later in the driveway of University President William Boyd.

42

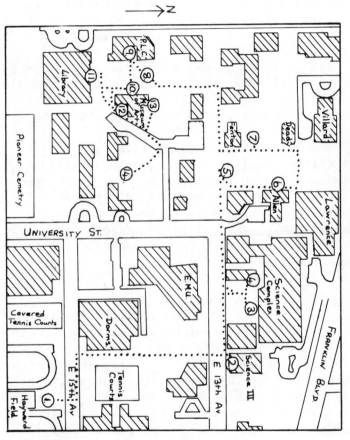

A University Art Walk

43

From here you can see the northeast wall of
the Vulcanology Building. There, slowly being
covered by moss, are 4 panels of scientific
symbols (4), the work of Spokane artist Harold
Balazs.

Now go back to 13th Street, turn right, and
keep walking, past the Geology Building, the traffic barricades, past Friendly Hall, into the large
courtyard on your right, just across 13th Street
from Johnson Hall.

It is interesting, though it has little to
do with art, that you can walk down the middle
of this part of 13th Street without fear of
being killed by a car. The Eugene City Council
waffled for more than 25 years over requests
by the University to close this part of 13th
Street to traffic. In the spring of 1970
students forced the issue by erecting barricades.
Late night assaults by enraged citizens of
Eugene and Springfield failed to remove the
barricades. Eventually, the Eugene City Council
okayed the closing and this section of 13th Street
became a walkway and a sometime scene of student
fairs.

The bronze statue near the center of the
courtyard is one of three works by Alexander
Phimister Proctor that we will see today. This
one, called The Pioneer (5) by Proctor, is
known to the University community as the Pioneer
Father. He strides resolutely forward, westward, you may think, until you walk to the base
of the statue and follow his gaze with your
own. Look right through the glass doors in
Johnson Hall and you will see that the Pioneer
Father has his gaze fixed on the Pioneer Mother,
whom we shall meet later in our walk, and that
he is striding forth to meet her. Do you suppose, on those moonlit summer nights, at the
time when tin soldiers come to life and Teddy
bears talk, that these two romantic old souls
might get together?

44

Onward. Our next stop is Allen Hall, which houses the School of Journalism and the Washington Hand Press, which printed the first newspaper west of the Missouri River.

On the outside of the west wall of Allen Hall are nine panels (6) carved with historically significant devices of publishers and typographers. Reading from north to south, they are:

1. Watermark, Pavia, Italy, 1453. This tulip device is typical of the simple designs of early watermarks.

2. Fust and Schoeffer, Mainz, Germany, 1457. The cross and V are derived from printers' rules. Fust and Schoeffer were successors to Johann Gutenberg. They were the first to print with movable type.

3. William Caxton, Westminster (London), England, 1475. Caxton was the first English printer. This design is based upon his monogram.

4. Englehard Schultis, Lyon, France, 1491. The acorn and monogram design was used by Schultis, an early printer in Lyon.

5. Octavanus Scotus, Venice, Italy, 1493. Venice was the printing center of Italy between 1481 and 1500. The double cross and orb design with monogram was used by Scotus, who was printing in Venice at that time.

6. Aldus Manutius, Venice, Italy, 1495. Manutius, was one of the most famous of the Italian printers. He was noted for designing Italic type faces.

7. Philippe le Noir, Paris, France, 1514. Philippe le Noir was the son of one France's earliest printers, Michel le Noir. His mark differed only slightly from his father's.

8. Frederick W. Goudy, American (1865-1947). Goudy established the Village Press at Park Ridge, Illinois, in 1903. The pegasus device is a well-known symbol of poetic inspiration.

9. John Henry Nash, San Francisco, (1871-1947). Nash was one of America's outstanding printers.

He once operated his press at the University of Oregon. This is one of his watermarks, which he designed using his initials.

Directly behind you as you contemplate the carvings on the side of Allen Hall is Deady Hall, the oldest building on the campus. It has been in continuous use since it opened in 1876, and, for the first ten years of its existence, it was the entire University. The bricks used to build Deady Hall were made of clay dug from the present site of McArthur Court.

The second oldest building on campus, Villard Hall, is to your right as you look at Deady Hall. It was completed in 1886.

Now, take the walkway back to 13th Street, on the Deady Hall side of the quadrangle. You will pass the Fenton Fountain (7), a gift to the University of the class of 1913.

Turn right when you get to 13th Street and walk until another wide, grassy quadrangle opens across the street on your left. Cross 13th Street and walk toward the University of Oregon Library, that large brick building facing you across the grass.

Conspicuous in the quadrangle is a yellow metal sculpture. Titled Reflections of a Summer Day (8), this sculpture was donated to the University in 1974 by the sculptor, Duane Loppnow, an alumnus of the University. Reflections of a Summer Day always reminds me of a collection of characters from an oriental alphabet.

If you are still facing the University Library, the building on your right is Prince Lucien Campbell Hall (PLC), on your left, the University of Oregon Museum of Art.

In the courtyard of PLC is a bronze sculpture, The Falconer (9), a 1974 gift of Jordan Schnitzer, given as a tribute to three of his English professors.

Stand near The Falconer and look across the quad at the Museum. From here the imposing Italian Romanesque style of the museum building can

46

be seen. The corbelled cornice band, the artistry in the brickwork, and the delicate artwork of the entryway are particularly appropriate for a museum of art.

Directly in front of the Museum, before the doorway, is the second of the Proctor sculptures that we will see today. Indian Maiden and Fawn (10) is a 1929 Proctor work, given to the University in 1962 by the estate of Narcissa J. Washburne. This is a delicate and graceful sculpture. The Indian maiden is gentle and lovely, but Proctor also captured something of the strength and stoicism of her race. She is feeding a delicate fawn. The naturalness of the young woman and the small fawn seems to symbolize a oneness of life, a unity between wildlife and mankind.

The University of Oregon Museum of Art (see entry, this chapter) is open from noon to five p.m., Tuesday through Sunday.

Now, walk back to the center of the quadrangle and look up at the library. The University of Oregon Library was built in three stages. The first, which faces the quadrangle, was completed in 1937. A Public Works Administration project, its general architectural style is modified Lombardic. As you look at the front of the Library, you will notice a decorative repeating pattern of cast stone heads (11). The heads are the work of Edna Dunberg, who completed only ten of them before she died in 1936 at the age of 23. The remaining five heads are by Jean Sutherland and Louis Utter Pritchard. The 15 famous men depicted on the front of the Library are: St. Thomas Aquinas, Aristotle, John Locke, Thucydides, Buddha, Jesus Christ, Michelangelo, Beethoven, Leonardo da Vinci, Sir Isaac Newton, Charles Darwin, Thomas Jefferson, Oliver Wendell Holmes, William Shakespeare, and Dante Alighieri.

Walk toward the library but angle off to your left, circling around behind the Museum of Art.

Just behind the Museum you will find The Family
Group (12), a stone sculpture that symbolizes
strength, unity, and love of a family together.
This sculpture, by Jonn Geise, was donated in
1974 as a Centennial gift to the University by
the William A. Haseltine family as a tribute
to Karl D. Unthank, a member of the faculty from
1909 until 1957.

Keep walking around the Museum, first on
the walkway and then on the grass, to the north
side. There you will find Prometheus (13), a
bronze sculpture by University faculty member
Jan Zach. This is indeed a hellish work, a con-
tinuation of the diabolical theme of some of
Zach's scupture in the Park Blocks downtown
(see "A Downtown Art Walk", this chapter).

If you are still facing Prometheus and the
Museum of Art, turn to your left and follow
the walkway toward the Erb Memorial Union.
Our next stop is our last.

On the grass to your right is the Pioneer
Mother (14), the last of the works by Alexander Phimister Proctor on today's Art Walk.
She appears to be grimly contemplating something
she has just read in a book, undoubtedly a
Bible, in her lap. I'd rather believe that
she's trying to figure out how she can gracefully get off that high marble base and go to meet
the old bronze gentleman who keeps eyeing her
through the glass doors from the other side
of Johnson Hall.

The Pioneer Mother was commissioned by
Burt Brown Barker, then University vice president,
as a memorial to his mother. Proctor completed
the sculpture in 1930 and Brown presided at the
dedication ceremonies in 1932. The three bronze
plaques set into the marble base were also cast
by Proctor.

Our art walk ends here. If you're still in
a walking mood, you might stroll through the Pioneer
Cemetery (see "Eugene's Old Cemeteries", Chapter

1) or, if you're hungry, you can find refresh-
ment in the Erb Memorial Union or at the Collier House (see Chapter 5).

There is much to see and experience on this
campus. I hope the art walk has provided you with
an enjoyable hour or two.

* *

A Downtown Art Walk

We will begin our downtown art walk in the
lobby of the Citizens Bank Building on the corner
of 10th & Oak Streets.

On the wall facing 10th Street hangs a large
tapestry (1) woven by Donna McGuinness, a
Eugene weaver. The tapestry is about 10' by
26', weighs over 300 pounds, and nearly covers
the large wall. It is so large that it should
be seen from afar to be fully appreciated. The
Note Counter prevents the viewer from gaining
that necessary perspective, but the dramatic
use of warm colors and the round, soft texture
of this massive piece o. art adds a great deal
of character and friendliness to what, without
the wall-hanging, would be just another ster-
ile bank lobby.

Leave the bank on the Oak Street side,
the side opposite tne parking lot, cross Oak
Street, and walk down the alley by KT's Sandwich Shoppe to the back door of the Broadway.

Over the staircase in the Broadway hangs a
strange and beautiful chandelier (2). "Everyone thought it was Hallowe'en when we got it,"
says the saleslady. "It looks like it ought
to have little hobgoblins coming out of it."

This is the work of Eugene metal sculptor
Ken Scott. It hangs by heavy chains from an
open beam in the ceiling and looks like two
branches of a gold and black tree, perhaps from
a fantastic forest where trees come alive in the

49

night and reach out to grab little travellers.
The light bulbs are encased in a fairy fruit
that hangs from the branches. They seem to be
part bell, part flower, and maybe the bottom
part is fashioned after the skirt that Cinderella wore to dance with the prince. In a way,
it seems almost alive, like a basket of snakes,
even in mid-day. I'll try to get back down the
stairs before it grabs me.

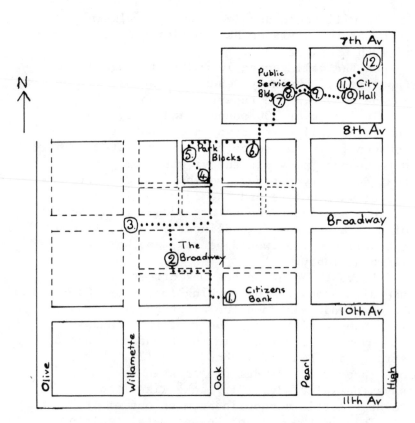

A Downtown Art Walk

That was some chandelier. Now, leave the
Broadway by the front door and turn left. Directly in front of you will be the center of
Eugene's downtown mall and the central fountain (3).

The fountain was designed by Hugh Mitchell,
now of Portland, as part of the overall mall design. It sits over a reservoir of approximately
10-12,000 gallons of water that is continually re-
circulated through the fountain. Often referred
to as a monument to the concrete industry, it
has the permanent look of something that will
still be here after the rest of our civilization
has turned to dust. It is easiest to appreciate
the mall fountain on those very cold winter days
when it is coated with ice.

Okay, about face and walk back down the mall.
A left at the First National Bank will take you
half a block along Oak Street to the Park Blocks.

In the center of the large fountain in this
tiny city center park, you will see a flight of
steel fish (4) skimming across the top of the
water. In the winter, on those rare cold days
when the sun shines brightly from a clear blue
sky, these fish are coated with ice, each in its
own halo, reflecting sunlight into shadows cast
by the large fir trees. This is the work of
Portland Sculptor Tom Hardy.

At the northwest corner of the park blocks
are three cast iron statues (5), the work of Eugene
sculptor Jan Zach. These sculptures might be,
depending on the fantasies of the viewer, three
raccoons in top hats, or three vandalized tree
stumps. They look decidedly gnomish to me,
standing at the edge of the park watching the
humans hustle about on their errands.

Now, walk east, across Oak Street, to the
other park block. Atop a wall near the fountain
are three more cast iron sculptures (6) by Zach.
These have a hellish aura about them, like flames
or thorns or some kind of Dantesque flower.

51

Directly across 8th Street from you now is the Lane County Courthouse and the Lane County Public Service Building(7). Thanks to a funding formula that decreed that one and one-half per-cent of all building costs, a sum of $110,000, would be spent for contemporary local art to be displayed in the building, the Lane County Public Service Building has become the showplace for Lane County art. There are 24 notable works of art by Lane County artists on permanent display in the Courthouse and the Public Service Building. Rather than guide you through the Court-house as I've done the University campus and the city streets, I'll list the artists and their works here and let you browse and react on your own. Pick up a directory at the Information Counter to find the exact location of each piece.

1. Cannery, an oil painting by Margaret Coe Clark.

2. Harbor at Florence, an oil painting by Joe Kelsey.

3. Oregon, a stainless steel sculpture by Jan Zach. This is notable because it is the most expensive of all the art works bought for the Public Service Building. The County paid $12,000 for this work.

4. Rivers, a bas relief wood sculpture by Paul Pearson.

5. Old Oregon House, a photograph by Paul Pearson.

6. Autumn Leaves, a photograph by Kim Harrington.

7. An unnamed water color by Jean Camille Ward.

8. A fabric flag by Margaret Matson.

9. Land Formation, an acrylic painting by Matt Clark.

10. Overpass, an oil painting by Eileen Duffy.

11. Two landscape tapestries by Glen Povey.

12. Woven diagonal stripe by Susan and Wayne Jewett.

13. An unnamed ceramic landscape by Michael Smith.

14. *Composition* I, a woven tapestry by Deri Cartier.

In the Lane County Courthouse:
1. Mosaic sculpture by Victoria Avakian Ross.
2. A mural by Howard Hall.
3. Mosaic by Robert James.
4. A metal sculpture by Phil Gilmore.
5. Paintings by Nelson Sandgren.
6. A mosaic by James Bartell.
7. A metal sculpture by Wayne Taysom.
8. A mosaic by Paul Tetzner.
9. A metal sculpture by Manuel Isguierdo.

After you've wandered around in the Public Service Building and the Courthouse, and maybe had something to eat in the cafeteria on the basement level, leave the Public Service Building via the east door, on the plaza level. Just before crossing the footbridge, notice the nine basalt rock forms in the plaza garden. This is called the Willamette Oracle Group (8), and was created by Dmitri Hadzi, sculptor-in-residence at Harvard University at the Oregon International Sculpture Symposium in the summer of 1974. Other works created during the Symposium can be seen in the park at the base of the bridges leading from Washington and Jefferson Streets to the I-105 freeway and in Alton Baker Park, where the Willamette Oracle Group originally resided.

Now we cross Pearl Street, via the footbridge, to the Eugene City Hall, where we will end our tour.

Directly in front of you as you step off the footbridge is another work of sculptor Jan Zach. Sometimes referred to as "tortured torsoes" (9), they are, according to a pamphlet available at the City Manager's Office, "...three women dressed in their best gowns to come to the town square, and are executed in a manner representing the great Oregon rivers, the McKenzie, the Willamette, and the Columbia. These figures are the largest single pour aluminum castings ever made in this country."

It is certain that something has been executed here, but I can't make them look like rivers or women. I do, however, get an impression, as I stand by these aluminum sculptures, of the artist, laughing all the way to the bank.

Inside the City Council Chambers, the round building behind the three tortured torsoes, is a large, garish mural (10). The mural, on the wall behind the City Council desk, is the work of Andrew Vincent, a Eugene painter. There is no unity to the mural though, according to the pamphlet, it represents scenes of old Eugene. It is an explosion of ill-chosen pastels from which the eye is repelled in all directions at the same time. The City Council has the advantage of not having to look at it during their meetings.

Much more to my liking is the wild fabric wall-hanging (11) in the rear of the Council Chambers. Commissioned for the Craftsmanship 1976, Eugene, Oregon show at the University of Oregon Museum of Art in 1976, the wall-hanging is the work of Barbara Neil, who now lives in Vancouver, British Columbia . It is a bright Byzantine Mandala with lettering at the bottom: EUGENE, OREGON, CENTER OF CRAFTS.

Our art walk ends in the northeast corner of the City Hall courtyard, at a large carved redwood log (12). According to the brochure, the log: "...represents a reclining figure done in a manner reminiscent of the rolling hills and valleys of Oregon..." Climb up onto the top of this log, as I did, and you will see

54

a sleeping totem pole. I'd like to see it standing
up, greeting visitors and glaring fiercely
across the courtyard instead of lying there,
a sleepy wooden giant.

Go on about your business in Eugene, a little
richer in knowledge of your city for having
taken this art tour.

✳ ✳

The University of Oregon Museum of Art

The University of Oregon Museum of art was
built in 1930. The architectural style is modified Italian Romanesque, and the repeating
pattern of four masks across the front of the
Museum represents the major art movements of the
world: Egyptian, Greek, Oriental, and Indian.

The Murray Warner Collection of Oriental
Art is housed in the Museum. It includes over
3200 objects representative of the cultures of
China and Japan. The collection is a gift,
given in 1921, of Mrs. Gertrude Bass Warner,
as a memorial to her husband, Major Murray
Warner. One of the outstanding features of the
Oriental collection is a 70-inch tall jade pagoda,
the largest assembled jade construction known
to exist. It was built in 1709 by Chinese artisans, and given to the Museum in 1957 by Winston
Guest. The Museum also houses a collection
of Manchu Dynasty court jewels, a collection of
Japanese Edo dolls (made in the 1500's) and the
Shiomi Collection of Oriental Art. Other out-

standing collections include the Haseltine
Collection of Contemporary Pacific Northwest Art, the Rolf and Alice Klep Collection,
and the works of Morris Graves.

On the first floor is a small gallery which
exhibits the work of contemporary photographers,
and two large galleries where the Museum maintains an extensive changing exhibition program,
including travelling exhibitions. The Museum
also has a rental-sales gallery and a gift
shop.

The Museum is open to the public Tuesday
through Sunday, 12 noon until 5:00 p.m., during
the school terms. Hours become erratic during
vacation periods and the Museum is closed from
mid-August until late September each year.

* *

The
Maude I. Kerns
Art Center

The Maude I. Kerns Art Center, located at
1910 East 15th Avenue, is a community art center.
Named for Maude I. Kerns, a Eugene artist and
art teacher who was the first benefactor of the
Center, it was incorporated as a non-profit
educational institution in 1953. The center's
main gallery is housed in the oldest existing
church building in Eugene.

The Center provides gallery space in the
Henry Korn Gallery for rotating exhibits of works
by locally and nationally known artists and

craftsmen.

It offers classes in the fine and applied arts, all taught by professional artists. Courses include ceramics, stained glass, photography, jewelry, painting, drawing, printmaking, and fibre arts.

For more information on the Maude Kerns Art Center, call 345-1571.

* *

Art Galleries

The following galleries, some of which are located in Eugene businesses, host rotating displays of art work.

The Bruinier Gallery of Student Photography
University of Oregon Library
Audiovisual Media Center
8 to 10 , Monday through Thursday
8 to 6 on Friday

Emerald Empire Art Center
421 North A Street
Springfield
11 to 4, Monday through Friday

Eugene Good Samaritan Center
3500 Hilyard Street
9:30 to 8, every day

Gallery 30
2650 Willamette Street
10 to 5, Tuesday through Saturday
1:30 to 4:30 Sunday

Gallery 141
Room 141, Lawrence Hall
University of Oregon
9 to 5, Monday through Friday

High Street Coffee Gallery
1243 High Street
7 a.m. to midnight, Monday through Friday
9 a.m. to 1 a.m. Saturday
10 to 10   Sunday

Lane Community College
Fine and Applied Arts Gallery
8 a.m. to 10 p.m., Monday through Thursday
8 to 5 Friday

Northside Gallery
North side of Franklin Boulevard
next to the bicycle path
Noon to 5, Monday through Friday

Open Gallery
445 High Street
11 to 5, Tuesday through Saturday

Opus 5 Gallery of Crafts
2469 Hilyard
11 to 5, Monday through Saturday

Solid Ingenuity
376 E. 11th
11 to 5:30, Monday through Friday
11 to 4 Saturday

Steven J.
941 Oak Street
9:30 to 5:30, Monday through Saturday

Susan Cummins Design Innovations
Smeede Hotel, Room 204
11 to 4, Monday through Friday

Original Graphics Gallery
122 E. Broadway
11 to 5:30, Tuesday through Saturday

Eugene Public Library
13th & Olive
10 to 9, Monday through Thursday
10 to 6 Friday and Saturday
1 to 5 Sunday

* *

Theater

    Theater groups spring up in Eugene with
amazing frequency. Some of them exist long enough
to do one or two plays and then quietly disappear.
What follows is a list of theater organizations
that will be performing in Eugene on a fairly
permanent basis. For information on current
productions of these and other, less permanent,
theater organizations, consult the Entertainment
Calendar in each Thursday's Register Guard or
the Calendar in the Living Well section of each
week's Willamette Valley Observer.

Oregon Repertory Theater
The Atrium, Second Floor
99 West 10th
485-1946

Very Little Theater
2350 Hilyard
344-7751

Pocket Playhouse and
Robinson Theater
University of Oregon Campus
686-4191

Performing Arts Department Theater
Lane Community College
726-2202 or 726-2209

Eugene is also fortunate to have excellent drama departments in several of its high schools. For information on high school drama offerings in your area, call:

Churchill High School	687-3421
North Eugene High School	687-3261
Sheldon High School	687-3381
South Eugene High School	687-3201
Willamette High School	689-0731
Marist High School	686-2234

* *

Libraries

University of Oregon

The largest library in Oregon, with over a million volumes, is the Main Library on the University of Oregon campus. The University has four other libraries: the Law School Library, with over 78,000 volumes; the Science Library, with more than 127,000 volumes; the School of Architecture and Allied Arts Library, with over 12,000 volumes; and the University of Oregon Map Library.

These libraries are available to University of Oregon students and to holders of town patron cards. Town patron cards are available to people who have identification with a local address, are out of high school, and who can supply the University with names and addresses

of three people who will always know where they
are. In addition, holders of certain other
library cards enjoy reciprocal privileges at
the University of Oregon Library.
For more information, call the Library
at 686-3065.

Lane Community College

Lane Community College has one main library
with more than 50,000 volumes. The LCC library
can be used by LCC students and holders of town
patron cards. Applicants for an LCC town patron
card must show proof of Lane County address and
a Social Security number.
For more information about the Lane Community
College Library, call 747-4501.

Eugene Public Library
100 West 13th

The Eugene Public Library has more than 200,000
books and records available for loan to library
patrons. Eugene residents may receive a library
card without charge. People who live outside
the city pay an annual fee for library use.
The Eugene Public Library sponsors many services and programs, including a Bookmobile that
brings the library to Eugene neighborhoods and
to homebound Eugene residents, puppet shows for
children on some Saturday mornings, story times
for children twice a week, and a Dial-a-Story
line (485-5511) for children.
For more information about the Eugene Public
Library, call 687-5450.

Lane County Pioneer Museum Library
Lane County Fairgrounds

The Museum Library occupies a corner of the

Lane County Pioneer Museum. It collects and
makes available to the public materials relat-
ing to the history of Lane County and its inhabitants. Photographs, portraits, manuscripts,
books and other printed materials, Lane County
archives, microfilm, tapes, newspapers, maps,
clippings, scrapbooks and local ephemera are
all available for use in the Library.

Eugene Register Guard
975 High Street

The Eugene Register Guard maintains a
library of stories written by Register Guard
reporters. Though it exists mainly as a
service to Register Guard reporters, it is
available for use by the public between
1:00 and 4:00, Monday through Friday.
For more information, call 485-1234.

Cascadian Regional Library
454 Willamette Street

The Cascadian Regional Library is not a
library in the usual sense. It is a clearing-
house for information on innovative projects
throughout the Pacific Northwest. The Library's
services fall into two main areas: Event Services,
such as planning and organizing fairs and con-
ferences; and Information Networking, which includes the development of information networks
among groups, production of mailing lists,
research, planning, and publishing.
For more information about the Cascadian
Regional Library, call 485-0366.

* *

Music and Dance

Numerous recitals are held throughout the year by the many schools of dance and music in Eugene. For information about recitals, see Thursday night's Register Guard, the Entertainment Calendar, or each week's calendar in the Willamette Valley Observer.

Community Center for the Performing Arts (CCPA)
Formerly the Woodsmen of the World (WOW) Hall
291 West 8th

The CCPA is in its fourth year of existence. Formerly the WOW Hall, the Center is owned and governed by a non-profit corporation. In the past three years the CCPA has hosted 75 national touring artists and 250 local artists, and has provided classes to more than 1500 students. Of 33 dance performances in Eugene between July, 1978, and February, 1979, by eight touring and five local companies, 14 were held at the CCPA.

For information about performances at the CCPA, see the publications mentioned above, or call 687-2746.

Beall Hall and
Robinson Theater
University of Oregon campus

Beall Hall is in use almost nightly during the time when the University is in session, as the scene of recitals by the University's Music School faculty and students, and for performances by touring artists. Robinson Theater is used less often, but is occasionally the scene of dance and music performances.

For information on performances on the
University of Oregon campus, call 686-4636.
Your call will activate a recording that lists
all the day's campus events.

Performing Arts Department Theater
Lane Community College

   The Performing Arts Department Theater at
Lane Community College is the scene of four
major musical performances during the year.
In addition, there are several other performances
scheduled throughout the year.
   For more information on performances at
LCC, call 726-2202 or 726-2209.

* *

Film

   In addition to Eugene's many theaters,
the University of Oregon schedules a profusion
of first-rate films, both foreign and domestic,
old and new, thoughout the school year. Films
at the University are an entertainment bargain,
as they usually cost $1.00 for admission. For
information on films at the University of
Oregon, call 686-4636 for a recorded message
containing all the day's campus events.
   Eugene's downtown theaters are much like
movie theaters everywhere, with the exception of
Cinema 7 in the Atrium Building at 99 W. 10th
Street. Cinema 7 features classic Hollywood
films and foreign films. Admission to Cinema
7 is the least expensive admission in Eugene,
$2.50, and, if you are a member of the Eugene
Film Society, ($5.00 for one year) admission to
Cinema 7 films is only $2.00.

* *

Lectures

The University of Oregon and Lane Community College offer lectures by authorities in their respective fields throughout the school year. These are usually announced well in advance in the Register Guard, the Willamette Valley Observer, the University of Oregon's Emerald, or the LCC Torch. Additional information may be had by calling the University's information line, 686-4636 or 686-3111, or the Lane Community College information line, 726-2201.

✶ ✶

Museums

Museum of Natural History
Science Building
University of Oregon

The University of Oregon Museum of Natural History has developed around the nucleus provided by Thomas Condon's collection of Oregon fossils. It is primarily a research department devoted to studies of the history of the earth, plants, animals, and man in Oregon.

Museum programs include displays, publication of research data, a public school loan program, a museum information service, and loans to other institutions. It is the official state depository and it maintains a large collection of fossils, plants, animals, rocks, and objects used by aboriginal man.

The Museum is open from 10 to 3, Monday through Friday.

The Butler Museum of American Indian Art
1155 West 1st Street
345-7055

The Butler Museum of American Indian Art houses
one of the largest collections of American Indian
art in Oregon. Its collection features baskets,
pottery, clothing, weaving, jewelry, and carvings from all the major culture areas of the
North American Indian.
The Museum is open from 10 to 5, Tuesday
through Saturday.

Lane County Pioneer Museum
740 W. 13th Avenue
687-4239

The Lane County Pioneer Museum houses a
large collection of items used by Lane County
pioneers. Items on display include clothing,
covered wagons, stage coaches, toys, tools,
furniture, and other memorabilia donated to
the Museum so that future generations could
visualize the life style of the pioneers.
The mission of the Lane County Pioneer Museum
is to collect, preserve, and interpret the
early history of Lane County.
The Museum is open from 9 to 5, Monday
through Friday, and from 1 to 5 on Saturday
and Sunday.

Willamette Science and Technology Center
(formerly SWOMSI)

At this writing, the Willamette Science and
Technology Center (formerly Southwest Oregon
Museum of Science and Industry, SWOMSI) is
building a new facility in Alton Baker Park.

The new building, which is scheduled to open during the summer of 1979, will house the largest planetarium in the Pacific Northwest.

Almost Everybody Runs in Eugene

Athletic Eugene:

A Guide to Sports and Recreation in the Track Capital of the World

Athletic Eugene:
A Guide to Sports and Recreation
in the Track Capital of the World

If you haven't seen someone running
yet, you've probably been in Eugene less
than ten minutes. Eugene is Tracktown,
USA, the place where jogging began in
America, the only city to host the U. S.
Olympic Trials three consecutive times.
Physical fitness is a way of life in
Eugene. Bike paths and jogging trails a-
bound. Playing fields and gymnasiums
are in constant use. If you have a favorite sport, there is undoubtedly a place
in Eugene where you can play it or watch
it.

Participant
Sports

Running and Jogging

If you're an avid runner, or just an occasional jogger, you're sure to have plenty of company
in Eugene. Eugene's streets echo round the clock
to the sound of runners' feet and, even if you
choose three a.m. as the time to work a run
into your daily routine, you're sure to pass
someone else who has chosen the same time for
his or her daily run.

The supreme running facility in Eugene is

Pre's Trail and Parcourse in Alton Baker Park.
Named for former University of Oregon runner
Steve Prefontaine, Pre's Trail is 6.3 kilometers
of wood chip running paths that cut through
filbert orchards along the banks of the Alton
Baker Park Waterway and the Willamette
River. The Parcourse is a loop with six exer-
cise stations. Though vandalism seriously crip-
pled the lighting effort along the trail during
the winter of 1978-79, there are lamps for the
entire length of the trail which are intended
to keep it lit and in use all night long.

In 1978 the City of Eugene installed a
similar running path, 1.6 kilometers long in
Amazon Park in south Eugene.

Other popular running routes include the
bike paths that border the Willamette River as
it passes through the city. The loop from the
Greenway Bicycle Bridge to the Autzen Stadium
Bicycle Bridge is 8.9 kilometers. From Alton
Baker Park to Valley River Center is 2.5
kilometers. The total distance of the North
Bank Trail, from Valley River Center to the
Springfield city limits, is 6.8 kilometers.

Though these facilities are available, runners
in Eugene do not feel confined to them. In Eugene
it's okay to run almost anywhere, and runners
are frequently seen striding through the downtown mall or passing quickly through the alleys
and streets in Eugene's residential areas.
Running for fun, for health, for fitness, is a
way of life in Eugene.

Tennis

In addition to the tennis courts on the
University of Oregon campus, which are nominally
reserved for members of the University community
but used by everyone, there are city-owned courts

71

available at the following locations: Amazon
Park, on the south side of 24th Avenue between
Amazon Parkway and Patterson Street; Echo Hollow
Park, 1655 Echo Hollow Road; Sheldon Community
Center, 2445 Willakenzie Road; Sladden Park,
North Adams and Cheshire Street; Westmoreland
Park, between 18th and 24th Streets on Polk
Street.

There are also tennis courts at Lane Community
College and at Churchill High School which may
be used by the public when classes are not in
session.

The following private organizations have tennis courts for use by members only: Eugene Swim
and Tennis Club, 66 Crescent, 344-4414; the YMCA,
2055 Patterson,344-6251; Eugene Elks Lodge,
2727 Centennial Boulevard, 345-8416.

Swimming

The Eugene Parks and Recreation Department oper-
ates the following swimming pools: Amazon (sum-
mers only), 2600 Hilyard Street, 687-5350;
Echo Hollow, 1655 Echo Hollow Road, 689-1831;
Jefferson Memorial, 16th Avenue and Jefferson
Street, 687-5352; Sheldon, 2445 Willakenzie Road,
687-5314.

The following organizations operate swimming
pools for members only. Eugene Swim and Tennis
Club, 66 Crescent, 344-4414; the YMCA, 2055
Patterson Street, 344-6251; Eugene Elks Lodge
No. 357, 2727 Centennial Boulevard, 345-8416.

A scuba diving course is offered by Eugene
Skin Divers Supply, Inc., 1090 West 6th Street,
342-2351. Scuba courses are also taught occasionally by the Parks Department, Lane Community
College, and the YMCA.

Flag Football

The Eugene Parks and Recreation Department sponsors a flag football league each fall. For information, call 687-5333.

Rugby

The Eugene Rugby Club practices on Thursday afternoons on the football field behind South Eugene High School. They schedule matches with other Pacific Coast rugby clubs, including the University of Oregon rugby club. For information, call Doug Craig at 686-2911.

Softball and Baseball

The Eugene Parks and Recreation Department sponsors men's, women's, and co-ed softball leagues for adults. For information on adult softball leagues, call 687-5333.

The Eugene Sports Program sponsors baseball and softball programs for boys and girls in grades 3 to 9. For information on ESP baseball and softball, call 683-2373.

Skiing

When it rains in Eugene, it's probably snowing in the Cascades. Because of Eugene's convenient location close to the Cascades, skiing is a favorite winter sport. Radio stations KUGN, KBDF, and KATR broadcast daily ski reports during the winter. Information is also available by calling the following telephone numbers: Hoodoo Ski Bowl, 345-7416; KBDF Ski Information Line, 343-7669; and Mt. Bachelor Ski Report, 344-7457.

The following Eugene merchants sell and rent

ski equipment and are good sources of information
about both downhill and cross-country skiing in
the Cascades: Hawkeye's the Good Life, 1290
Oak, 345-6665; Berg's Nordic Ski Shop, 410 E.
11th, 683-1100; Sugar Pine Ridge, 875 E. 13th,
345-5584.

Fishing

A day trip from Eugene can take you to a
high mountain lake where you might catch a
mess of trout, or out into the Pacific Ocean on
a charter boat to fish for salmon. Eugene is so
close to the McKenzie River that many people
leave after work, fish the McKenzie for a
couple of hours, and still get home in time for
dinner. In recent years, due to the clean-up
of the Willamette River, trout and salmon have
been taken from the Willamette inside the Eugene
city limits. Fishing is an easy, inexpensive, and
popular pastime of people in Eugene.

Information on charter fishing trips from
Winchester Bay is available from the following
places: Main Charters, 271-2800; Shamrock Charters, 271-3232; Winchester Bay Sport Fishing
Boats, 271-3702.

Newport Sport Fishing, Inc. can take you
on a charter fishing trip from Newport. For
information, call 265-7558.

If you are interested in fly fishing, the
following merchants can supply all of your needs:
The Caddis Fly Angling Shop, 450 Willamette,
342-7005; The Fly Fisherman's Bookcase and
Tackle Service, 3890 Stewart Road, 485-6775.

The best prices on fishing gear are found
annually at Bi-Mart during their pre-fishing
season sale.

Hiking, Backpacking Camping

The Cascade Mountains provide hikers and

backpackers with wilderness and mountain-top experiences year-round. Maps and other information on wilderness areas and forest recreation opportunities are available at the headquarters of the Willamette National Forest in the Federal Building in Eugene, or from any ranger district headquarters. For information on appropriate equipment, I recommend Berg's, 11th & Mill, 683-1100; or Mattox Outdoor Outfitters, 57 West Broadway, 686-2332.

Canoeing, Boating, Rafting

The millrace on the south side of the Willamette River and the canoe run in Alton Baker Park are popular places for canoeing in Eugene. Better canoers do their thing on the Willamette. Canoes can be rented from the University of Oregon canoe shack on the millrace across Franklin Boulevard from the Science Building, or from the canoe concession on the canoe run in Alton Baker Park. Canoe rental on the millrace is less expensive than from the canoe concession in the park.

If this sounds too tame for you, maybe you'd like to run a wild river. River Expeditions (689-7923) will take you 48 miles down the McKenzie in a rubber raft. Wayne Gardner, a Leaburg river outfitter and guide, (896-3215) will take you down just about any river you might want to try.

Bicycling

The Department of Public Works in City Hall II, 858 Pearl Street, has an excellent free map of all of Eugene's bike paths. For expert bicycle service, I recommend Collins Cycle Shop, 60 E. 11th, 342-4878.

For more on bicycling in Eugene, consult the bicycling section of Chapter 9.

Golf

Golf is a year-round sport in Eugene. Here is a list of eight golf courses, open to the public, within 30 minutes driving time of Eugene's downtown area: Emerald Valley Golf Course, 83293 Dale Kuni Road, Creswell, 484-6354; Greenacres Golf Course, 1375 Irving Road, 688-1005. Fiddler's Green Golf Course, 91292 Highway 99N, 689-8464; Hidden Valley Golf Course, 775 N. River Road, Cottage Grove, 042-3046; Laurelwood Municipal Golf Course, 2700 Columbia, 687-5321; McKenzie River Golf Course, Leaburg, 896- 3454; Oakway Golf Course, 2000 Cal Young Road, 484-1927; Springfield Country Club, 90545 Marcola Road, Springfield, 747-2517.

Soccer

Soccer is growing rapidly in popularity in Eugene, for players of all ages.

The American Youth Soccer Organization (688-0946) and the Eugene Sports Program (683-2373) sponsor soccer leagues for elementary school boys and girls. District 4J schools field teams for scholastic competition in the junior high schools and in the high schools. The Eugene Parks and Recreation Department (687-5333) sponsors city league competition for adults.

Competitive Running

There are marathons and runs scheduled through-the year in and around Eugene, including the Nike-Oregon Track Club Marathon in September. During the summer the Oregon Track Club hosts weekly all-comers meets at Hayward Field on the University of Oregon campus. The Athletic Department, in the Atrium Building at 10th and Olive (342-5155) and Sugar Pine Ridge, 875 E. 13th (345-5584) are good

places to find information on upcoming runs
and to talk with people who know about running.

Basketball

Basketball, like soccer, is played by people
of all ages in Eugene. The Eugene Sports Program
(683-2373) and the YMCA (344-6251) sponsor competition for elementary school age boys and girls.
District 4J schools field teams for high school
and junior high school competition, and the
Eugene Parks and Recreation Department (687-5333)
sponsors city league competition for adults.

Ice Skating

It's done on plastic, but it's like ice skating.
The iceless ice skating arena is the Magic Skate
Ice Arena, 77 W. 11th, 484-5272.

Roller Skating

Roller skaters in Eugene do it on the side-
walk or go to the following roller rinks: Big
Wheel Skate Center, 333 River Avenue, 688-6633;
Kreklau's Roller Rink, 5300 Fox Hollow Road,
344-2989; or Skate World, 3188 Gateway Loop,
Springfield, 485-5272.

Women's Field Hockey

University of Oregon women interested in
playing women's field hockey should contact
Nancy Plantz in the Athletic Department at
the University. Women not affiliated with
the University who are interested in playing
field hockey for the Eugene Hockey Club should
contact Georgia Cutler at Churchill High School
or call her at 344-5864.

Bowling

Eugene is well supplied with bowling lanes. In addition to the bowling lanes in the basement of the Erb Memorial Union at the University of Oregon, there are six bowling alleys in Eugene and Springfield. They are: Emerald Lanes, 40 Oakway Road, 342-2611; Fairfield Lanes, 1170 Pacific Highway 99N, 688-8900; Firs Bowl, 1950 River Road, 688-1558; Springfield Lanes, 205 Q Street, Springfield, 746-8292; Timber Bowl, 924 Main, Springfield, 746-8221; Webfoot Lane, 2486 Willamette, 345-8575.

Gymnastics

Eugene is the home of the Oregon Academy of Artistic Gymnastic, a nationally recognized training school for future Olympians. The Academy has won the national gymnastic team title for the past three years.

The Academy offers instruction to the public for children from age 5 through high school. For more information, call the Academy at 344-2001.

* *

Spectator Sports

University of Oregon

The University of Oregon provides the people of Eugene with the opportunity to watch some of the best NCAA sports action in the country. Three facilities belonging to the University of Oregon deserve special mention in this section:

<u>Hayward Field</u> and <u>Stephenson Track</u>. This track and field facility is one of the finest in the country. The Olympic trials were held here in 1972 and 1976, and will again be held here in

1980. It is largely because of Hayward Field
that Eugene has been awarded the Olympic Trials
an unprecedented three straight times. Hayward
Field is the site of the University of Oregon
NCAA competition and invitational meets sponsored by the Oregon Track Club during the
spring and, on Thursday afternoons in the
summer, all-comers meets are held there.

McArthur Court. This ancient facility is
the largest sports arena in Eugene. On basketball weekends during the winter it is filled to
capacity with "deranged idiots" who come to "the
Pit" to cheer the Ducks on to victory over their
Pacific Coast Conference rivals. For sheer
excitement there are few experiences that
match being in the Pit late in a close game
between Oregon and UCLA or Washington or Oregon
State, when the Pit throbs to the sound of the
Oregon Pep Band and 10,000 deranged idiots howl-
ing for an Oregon victory. Wrestling matches,
womens' basketball, and world class gymnastics
competitions are also held in the Pit.

Autzen Stadium. Located across the Willamette
River from the main campus, Autzen Stadium is
easily reached via a footbridge. The stadium
was built in 1967 and has a seating capacity
of 41,000. Because of uninspiring performances
by the University of Oregon football teams in
recent years, it is seldom filled to capacity.
During the football season, area high schools use
the stadium for Friday night doubleheaders.
University of Oregon games are played on Saturday afternoons.

For information about athletic events in-
volving University of Oregon teams, call the
University Athletic Event Information Line,
686-5241. For information about tickets, call
the ticket office at 686-4461. For other information about University of Oregon athletics,

call 686-4481.

Emerald Baseball

The Emerald Baseball Club, a farm team of the Cincinnati Reds, is the only professional sports organization consistently active in Eugene. The Ems play a full schedule with other Northwest League teams in the old Civic Stadium on Willamette Street. The season lasts from mid-June to the end of August. For more information about Emerald Baseball, call 342-5367.

Lane Community College

Though it has no football team, Lane Community College fields teams in most other sports. For information on Lane Community College athletic events, call the LCC Athletic Department at 726-2215.

High School Sports

For information about high school athletic events in Eugene, call School District #4J at 687-3123, or the Bethel School District at 688-8611.

* *

Eugene's
Parklands

Still looking for something to do? Go to a park.

Eugene has 69 park sites, a total of 1110.63 acres of park land, not including Alton Baker Park, which is in Eugene but belongs to Lane

80

County.

In a park in Eugene you can climb a mountain, feed a duck, catch a fish, lie in the sun, swim, swing, throw a frisbee or football or baseball, broil a hamburger over a charcoal fire, walk through a secluded wood, enjoy an explosion of colors in a rhododendren garden, pause to smell the roses in a huge rose garden, get married, ride a bike, ride a dinosaur, climb into a rocket, drive a fire engine, join a soccer or basketball game, rent a canoe and paddle along a waterway, listen to a rock band, toss horseshoes, or just sit under a tree and watch all the other people doing these things.

My kids like to go to swingset parks, their name for parks with play equipment. This kind of equipment is located at every elementary school in Eugene, and at the following parks:

Acorn Park
15th & Buck Streets

Amazon Park
27th & Hilyard Streets

Berkeley Park
3629 W. 14th Avenue

Country Lane Park
2975 Country Lane

Edgewood Park
4600 Hilyard Street

Fairmount Park
15th and Fairmount

Friendly Park
27th & Monroe Streets

Grant Park
10th and Grant Streets

Hendricks Park
Summit & Skyline Drive
(2 swings only)

Laurel Hill Park
E. 26th & Augusta

Milton Park
3300 University

Morse Ranch
595 Crest Drive

Petersen Park
3825 Royal Avenue

Skinner Butte Park
High to Lincoln
on Cheshire

Sladden Park
North Adams and Cheshire

South Amazon Park 36th-38th on Hilyard	University Park East 24th & University
States Streets Park Dakota and Burnett	Washington Park 19th-20th on Washington

...you are a Stranger to this far off west and those that inhabit it, and the beautiful scenes which surround us in Oregon but could you but see our land of enchantment...

Eugene Skinner
to his sister
March 18, 1860

From
the Mountains
to the Sea:

A Guide
to the Sights
In and Around
Eugene

Around
the Town—
A few Viewpoints

Spencer's Butte

As with the best of most everything else, the
best view of Eugene is not the easiest to gain.

From the top of Spencer's Butte, that massive
hill overlooking Eugene from the south, the view
of the city and the southern end of the Willamette
Valley is spectacular. From here, and only from
here, the earthbound can behold Eugene in the
context of our valley environment. All is visible.
The rich green fields and forests, the snowcapped
peaks of the Cascades to the east, the blue-
purple of the Coburg Hills to the northeast
and the rolling Coast Range to the west define
our end, the south end, the upper end, of the
Willamette Valley.

Eugene once nestled down there in the heart
of all that greenery. Now it sprawls across the
valley floor, its urban tentacles creeping
relentlessly along the highways that slash
up into the hills and mountains. Here comes the

McKenzie, there's the Willamette, almost roadlike in their tamed ramble down from the mountains. Out there is Fern Ridge Reservoir, a mud puddle in the giant field of our vision. Back behind us are Eugene's little cousins, Creswell and Cottage Grove.

To get to Spencer's Butte, just drive south on Willamette Street until you are about a mile or so beyond the city limits. Spencer Butte Park is marked by a large wooden sign on the left side of the road. Park in the parking lot and begin to climb. The walk to the top is steep. The trail is clearly marked until you are almost to the top. From there, just think "up" and you can't go wrong.

In the winter, when the fog lies thick over Eugene, or in the summer when the field-burning smoke thickens the air, you can walk up Spencer's Butte and breathe clean, clear air and see the mountains, see forever, it seems, over the top of the grey valley air. The view is especially worth the effort on these days. With a little stretch of the imagination you can almost see migrating whales spouting in the Pacific just beyond Florence.

Some things to remember:

1) Stick to the trail. Climbers who take shortcuts across the switchbacks destroy fragile vegetation, contribute to harmful erosion, and contract poison oak.

2) Pick up your garbage. Cigarette butts and sandwich wrappers and beer bottles are ugly reminders of our intrusion into this peaceful place.

3) Keep your dog on a leash. This may be a little wilderness, but it is also a very popular Eugene city park. Few things are more terrifying to a small child than for him or her to meet your bounding, slobbering, hyperactive 50-pound housepet when he or she is for a moment or two alone on a mountain trail.

Man is a guest on this wild little mountain.
Mind your manners.

Skinner's Butte

The second best view of Eugene is easily
accessible. A road will take you, car, family
and all, right to the top of Skinner's Butte
where a parking area adjoins what was once a
planetarium belonging to the University of
Oregon. From here you'll be able to look north,
right up Willamette Street to Spencer's Butte.
This is an especially lovely view in the early
evening, when the lights begin to twinkle on in
the city and the blocks and buildings fade into
the dusk. Later at night the top of Skinner's
Butte becomes Eugene's most popular lovers' lane.
    Just take High Street north through Skinner's
Butte Park and follow the road around the Butte
to the top.

South Hills

There are some spectacular views of the city
from the residential areas in the south hills,
especially on the hill above Fairmount Boulevard
as you drive toward Hendricks Park and branch
onto The Heights or onto Spring Boulevard, or as
you drive along University Street above East
and West Amazon.

Day Trips

Because of Eugene's location between
the snowy crags of the Cascades and the
thundering surf of the Pacific, a variety
of interesting day trips are possible.
They are exciting possibilities for any
time of year.

To the Sea

Eugene is just over 60 miles from one of
the most scenic areas of the Pacific Coast. If
you enjoy exploring tide pools, watching sea
lions, whales, seals, fishing boats, birds, or
roasting hot dogs and marshmallows over the coals
of a seaside driftwood fire, or if dramatic
cliffs and the wild spray of surf flinging
itself against massive boulders fills you with
awe, this trip is for you.

Head west on 11th Street. If you keep going
you'll drive through Veneta and Noti on Highway
126 to Florence, where the Siuslaw River enters
the Pacific Ocean. Often when the valley fills
with clouds, the sky here is clear, the wind
still, and the beaches warm. Unfortunately,
a weather pattern just the reverse of this is
common as well.

North of Florence, Highway 101 was carved
into the cliffs of Heceta Head, high above the
ocean. There are wide spots in this impossible
road where you can pull over, get out of the
car, and spit into the ocean--hundreds of feet
below. On a clear day you can see miles of waves
washing the beaches north and south of the headland. Migrating whales are often visible, some
very close to the cliffs, as they move along the
shore. Seals, sea lions, and a great number of
birds sometimes bob along in the surf or rest
easily on the rocks far below.

At Sea Lion Caves, about 12 miles north of
Florence, you can take an elevator down the
cliff to a cave where sea lions make their
home all year long.

Oregon State Parks are among the best, and
cleanest, in the United States. Along the coast
each of the state parks has a special appeal all
its own.

A couple of miles north of Sea Lion Caves,
Heceta Lighthouse overlooks Devil's Elbow State
Park.

Devil's Elbow is appropriately named, for
it is easy to be seduced right into the surf
here. Waves crash with devastating force
against the rocks where the headland trickles
into the sea, and the impulse of the visitor
is always to get a little closer, to experience
that terrible force up close. Nearly every
year at least one person gets just a little too
close and becomes a victim of the sneaky Pacific.

A path through the woods takes visitors
past the magnificent lighthouse caretaker's
house and on to the lighthouse. Heceta Lighthouse is no longer manned, but run by remote
control. The caretaker's house, said to be
haunted by the ghost of a lady who lived there
long ago, now belongs to Lane Community College.

Farther north are the Carl G. Washburne
Memorial State Park, and the Muriel O. Ponsler
Memorial Wayside. The offering here is a
long stretch of lonely beach, vast tranquil
places to walk among the driftwood, to let your
dog run or to picnic and contemplate the power
and size of the ocean.

Strawberry Hill State Park doesn't look like
much from the highway, but for anyone interested
in exploring tidepools or watching seals, this
is a fascinating place.

Park in the small parking lot behind the hill
and scramble down the path over the headland.
Here the ocean has carved tide pools and channels
into the rock and populated them with an assortment of seashore life that would delight anyone.
Sea anemones, barnacles, crabs, mussels, hermit
crabs, other shellfish, snails, many kinds of
seaweed, tiny fish and other seashore animals
and plants crawl, sway, lurch and dart along the
bottom of this watery wonderland. The channels
alternately swell with water and empty as the
waves come and go, their soughing, splashing,
sucking, slapping and slipping-away sounds adding
to the magic of this special place.

Keep going, over the rocks. When you have
gone as far as you can go without swimming, look
up and you'll be eye-to-eye with a dozen or more
seals. They loll about on the rocks across that
last and biggest channel before the ocean. Some
will undoubtedly slip into the ocean as you approach
but most will just raise their heads and stare
back at you, probably as interested in you as
you are in them.

After a moment you will notice that the seals
who slid into the ocean haven't gone far, that
they are probably watching you from the water,
bobbing gracefully along on top of the waves
and occasionally disappearing without a ripple,
only to pop up again in a moment or two and rivet
you again with their curious stare. Sea gulls and
cormorants, too, will be bobbing on the waves here,
or walking among the seals looking for grisly
tid-bits from which they can make a meal.

Be here at sunset on a clear day, and watch
the sun sink into the ocean under a bright pink
sky behind the lazy seals and the crashing surf.
There's magic on the Oregon coast at such a time.

Back in the car. Point it north again.
Neptune State Park is next, flat sand strewn
boulders big enough to provide shelter from the
wind. On a cold winter day, with the sun shining
from the clear blue sky, the wind stopped
by these huge rocks and a driftwood fire popping
and flaring in the sand, it is warm here. This
is a perfect place for a December or January
picnic, and a good example of the efficiency of
solar heating. Take a Frisbee, a foam rubber
football, some hot dogs, graham crackers, marshmallows, a couple of chocolate bars and a few
children, and you'll all have a memorable day at
Neptune State Park.

If the tide's far enough out you can clamber
onto the rocks just north of where you are pic-
nicking. Again, a mind-boggling variety of sea
life will greet you. A glistening little world
exists here on the edge of the sea.

If you have a large pot in your car--carry one for just such an emergency--pull some mussels loose from the rocks and boil them in sea water over your driftwood fire. Their shells will open in the hot water and you'll be able to pull the bright orange meat loose from the inside. Pop it into your mouth, the whole thing, wash it down with some good Blitz beer, and you will have experienced a truly Oregon treat.

Now it's time to make a decision. From Neptune Park you are about two hours from Eugene, and you could easily return to the city for the night. You could press on, though, north to Newport and then east through the Van Duzer Forest Corridor to Corvallis and back to Eugene on Highway 99. If you're in a hurty you'll want to retrace your steps. Completing the loop takes longer, but it's worth the extra time.

If you decide to go on, you'll again head north. Next on the list of things to see is the Cape Perpetua Recreation Area and Visitor's Center.

The Recreation Area features trails that take you from the seashore to the hills east of the highway. Along the trails are little signs that enlighten the visitor about his or her natural surroundings, commenting on everything from the giant Coast Range slugs to the berry bushes to erosion to the giant spruce tree in a canyon just beyond the camping area.

In the Visitor's Center you'll see audiovisual displays that explain much about the forest and the sea, including a Disney-type nature film shown in the Visitor Center theater. This is the longest-running film on the Oregon coast. Knowledgeable Forest Service employees are also on duty at the Center to answer questions. From the Visitor Center you can see over miles of ocean. It is a good place to watch ships and whales as the move up and down the coast.

Next, just before you enter the little
town of Yachats, is the Shamrock Lodgettes,
a good place to spend the night before completing the loop to Eugene the next morning.
At the Shamrock Lodgettes you will sleep in
squeaky clean and comfortable log cabins within
sight and sound of the ocean. The management
supplies plenty of firewood, so you can toast
your toes in front of the large stone fireplace
in your cabin. A glass of wine, a crackling fire,
the roar of the ocean--all at once is possible
at the Shamrock Lodgettes. Another small but nice
touch is that the management will deliver the
Salem evening newspaper to your door.

Across the Yachats River from the Shamrock
Lodgettes is the sleepy little town of Yachats.
The drive from Yachats (pronounced Ya-hots)
to Newport is through scrub coastal vegetation and,
except for the quaint town of Waldport and the
bridges that cross the Alsea and Yaquina Rivers,
it is a fairly uninteresting trip. A few attempts
have been made to develop some tourist attraction,
but they add only a cheap carnival effect to the
roadside scenery, marring rather than enhancing
their environment.

As you enter Newport you will see signs di-
recting you to the Oregon State University
Marine Science Center. Follow them.

The Marine Science Center houses a collection
of exhibits that explain various things about the
ocean, its vast number of living creatures, its
effect on our climate, economy, and ecology and
its incredible potential as an almost undeveloped
natural resource. There is also a live octopus
who may slip a suction-cupped tentacle out of his
tank to shake your hand and an exhibit of other
ocean creatures that children are encouraged to
handle--carefully. This is an excellent exhibit
and, if you invest the time to visit, the Marine
Science Center will become a highlight of your
trip.

Newport is a picturesque seaport, home for
a large fleet of ocean-going fishing boats.
Walk along the Newport waterfront and down onto
the docks for a close look at the boats. You will
also probably see people fishing or crabbing
from the docks and you may be tempted to walk
back into the town and rent a crab net for
yourself.

Leave Newport on Highway 20 to Toledo,
through the Coast Range and the Van Duzer Forest
Corridor, on down onto the flatness of the
Willamette Valley floor, and into Corvallis.
In Corvallis you may want to visit the campus of
Oregon State University before heading south on
Highway 99 to Eugene.

The most pleasant route back to Eugene is
to follow Highway 99 to Junction City, turn left
at Junction City's city-center traffic light, cross
the railroad tracks, then turn right to the
stop sign. Now turn left onto River Road and
follow it into Eugene. This route misses the
industrial sprawl of West Eugene and will take
you through bucolic farmland right to the city
limits.

Where to eat at the coast? Mo's. Until Mo's
opened in Florence there was nothing but disappoint-
ment awaiting the hungry visitor to that coastal
town. Now there is a Mo's in Florence and another
in in Newport, serving the same deliciously-pre-
pared fresh seafood in both places.

If you take the entire loop and you're not
sick of fish by the time you hit Corvallis,
you'll want to stop at the Tower of London for
the best fish and chips in Oregon.

Go North

This trip, north from Eugene on Highway 99W,
will take you through the agricultural heartland
of the Willamette Valley, let you picnic on the
fringe of the Coast Range on a 100-foot table cut

92

from the heart of one Douglas fir tree, observe the winter feeding ground for thousands of ducks and Canadian geese, tour the best of Oregon State University, and see thousands of quail and pheasants in the E. E. Wilson Game Management Area just north of Corvallis. Children and other lovers of wildlife and farm animals will delight in the profusion and variety of birds and animals that can be observed close at hand in the course of five or six hours of driving and walking.

Begin the trip on River Road in Eugene, and drive north to Junction City.

You could go to Junction City on Highway 99W, and you would probably get there a little sooner, but the drive out along River Road avoids the industrial sprawl of Eugene as it straggles north along the highway. Instead of fighting for the right-of-way with logging trucks and freightliners as they barrel single-mindedly along in a haze of exhaust fumes past lumber mills and cut-rate plywood dealers, enjoy a leisurely drive. River Road becomes a country lane, cutting through pastures and fields where, depending on the season, you may see rye grass, corn, beans, ming, wheat, turkeys, lambs, cattle, pumpkins, squash, strawberries, or many other agricultural products.

During the summer and fall this is the place to shop for fresh, inexpensive produce. Many of the farmers allow customers to pick their own produce and, just before Halloween, farmers along River Road open their pumpkin patches to people who want to choose their Jack O'Lanterns right off the vine. Shopping here for pumpkins and produce is less expensive and more fun than choosing from a pile of pumpkins or a little green box of strawberries at Albertson's.

At the stoplight in Junction City turn right, head north to the edge of town where the road forks and a large sign invites you to stop at

the Junction House. "Open," Promises the sign,
with large red letters. Look around. The Junction
House is gone. The sign remains, advertising a
phantom restaurant.

Take the left fork and you're once again
passing through bucolic agricultural scenery.
This area produces 90% of the rye grass seed
grown in America. If your nose is running and
your eyes itch as you pass through this grass-
land, it's spring, the grass fields are pollinat-
ing, and you have hay fever. If it seems dark
in the middle of the day, your eyes and nasal
passages sting, and everything smells smoky,
it's late summer and the farmers are burning their
fields and angering the clean-air advocates
in Eugene and Salem.

The Coast Range rises from the flat valley
floor to your left. On your right the Cascades
may be visible and, behind you on your right,
are the Coburg Hills.

Ten miles from Junction City a bridge spans
the Long Tom River at the edge of the little
town of Monroe. Just beyond the northern
edge of Monroe, a sign points left up a narrow
road that rises and falls with the hills, to the
even smaller town of Alpine. Go to Alpine,
then follow the signs to Bellfountain.

The villages, Alpine and Bellfountain, are
scenic little places where time seems to almost
stand still--gas station, grocery store, tavern
and church, nestled into little hollows on the
edge of the Willamette Valley and the edge of
the Coast Range.

Turn left at Bellfountain and follow the road
to the top of the hill. Where you find a large
old house on your left, turn right and you will
be in Bellfountain Park.

You will probably be the only people at the
park, and it will be quiet but for the sound of
a gentle wind in the trees. An amazingly large
slab of wood, cut from the heart of one tree,

94

forms a picnic table at which an entire tribe
of large people could sit, with ample room for
everyone's children and elbows. That huge table
is symbolic of the timber industry, one of
western Oregon's major industries. In your mind,
try to imagine the tree within which that
table grew.

Picnic here. Fling your football or Frisbee
over the lush grass. This place invites one to
run, to roll in the sweet-smelling grass, to
explore the forest on the side of the hill, to
look for frogs by the little spring in the
trees, or just to relax in a quiet and comfortable
place.

Go back to the village and turn north again.
This time the road takes you along the western
edge of the <u>William</u> <u>L.</u> <u>Finley</u> <u>National</u> <u>Wildlife</u>
<u>Refuge</u>, a favorite wintering area for thousands
of migrating waterfowl, including large and
noisy Canadian geese and several colorful varieties
of duck. Often you will see them circling
in formation like a flight of little bombers,
searching for a safe landing site, or standing
about in the grain fields as they eat.

Stop and turn off your engine. Listen.
You will hear them, thousands of waterfowl
voices, quacking, honking and squawking. This is
the sound of winter, approaching or receding,
in the Willamette Valley.

From here you can take any of several roads
to the right, east, to Highway 99W, or you can
follow this pleasant little road on north, to
<u>Philomath</u>. Either way, the next stop is <u>Corvallis</u>,
at <u>Oregon</u> <u>State</u> <u>University</u>.

Before you get to Corvallis, look to your
left. The highest of the series of Coast Range
peaks visible to you as you enter Corvallis is
<u>Mary's</u> <u>Peak</u>, 4097 feet above sea level, the
highest mountain in the Oregon Coast Range.

Oregon State University is one of the leading
agricultural universities in the nation. It
maintains experimental herds of cattle, sheep,

goats, pigs, and horses, flocks of turkeys and
chickens, on agricultural experiment stations
all over the state. Here, on the western edge
of the University campus, is the largest agricultural experiment station of all. Visiting
the barns at Oregon State University is like
visiting a large farm, but here is a variety of
farm animals that few private farms or ranches
can support.

My children, who are city-bound in Eugene
most of the year, are fascinated by occasional
trips to the barns at Oregon State. Early in
the spring, when the lambing occurs, visitors
can watch tiny lambs being suckled by their
mothers in the sheep pens. When a ewe is short
on milk, the lambs are bottle-fed by student
workers. There are cows and calves, enormous
bulls and steers, goats that butt the fence and
each other just for fun.

Pigs farrow all year round, so there is
always a show at the pig barns. A normal pig
litter is about 12, but at least one sow here
gave birth to 22 piglets in one litter. In
pen after pen, 500-pound sows lie on their sides
and gently suckle ten or so of their offspring.
The sight and sound of hundreds of piglets
grunting and squealing as they struggle for
access to their favorite nipples is interesting
and educational for young children and old
children alike. Surely no one who visits
these barns grows up believing that milk ori-
ginates in bottles of cardboard containers.

Oregon State University offers the visitor
much more, including a museum of natural history,
a historical museum, an occasional rodeo, dramatic performances, and the usual schedule of
Pac-10 athletic contests, but this is just a
Sunday outing and we must hurry.

Back on Highway 99, moving north once more.
Fifteen miles north of Corvallis is the
E. E. Wilson Game Management Area, experiments
are carried out by the Oregon State Department

of Fish and Game, on a large experimental population of quail and ring-necked pheasants, favorite game birds of Oregon hunters.

Little grey quail scurry about in bunches, top-knots erect. The ring-necked pheasant is a bird of great beauty, a dazzling array of bright greens and reds and browns. They strut proudly about their pens, crowing and preening themselves. This is a sight any bird-fancier or pheasant hunter would drive miles to see.

Now, one more state park. Sarah Helmick State Park is only a couple of miles north of here. Helmick is clean, quiet, and very pretty, another good place for a picnic or a leisurely stretch and run for all those who are tired of sitting in the car.

Okay, all of you, back in the car. It's time to head on home.

Back in Corvallis you'll want to stop for dinner--fish and chips at the Tower of London. The Tower is the best place in Oregon for fish and chips. Then, if you're not clear full, pick up an ice cream cone at Baskin & Robbins, just a couple of blocks away on your way back to Eugene.

In an hour you'll be back in Eugene, an interesting and enjoyable day behind you.

Go South

Though I've known of its existence for a long time, it was only because I was doing research for this book that I finally attempted to visit the Bohemia mining country.

Because it is written up in every Chamber of Commerce and AAA publication that have ever been put together about the Cottage Grove area, I expected a plasticized frontier town, overrun by tourists, something on the order of Disneyland. To my great delight, I found it

97

primitive and hard to get to. In fact, because
I went in February when the snow was still sitting on the upper elevations of Bohemia Mountain,
I couldn't get to the ghost town of Bohemia City,
even in a four-wheel drive vehicle. I'll be
back, though, when the snow melts.

To get to the Bohemia mining country, drive
south on Interstate 5 to Cottage Grove. Take
the first Cottage Grove exit, circle under the
freeway and drive east, past the office of the
Oregon State Police, toward the mountains.
Soon you will see signs pointing the way to the
Bohemia mining country.

As you drive along the Row River, you may
be discouraged, especially along the stretch of
road right after the village of Dorena, and
around the Bohemia Lumber Mill, because the humans who live along this lovely little river
have done so much to rob it of its beauty.
This ugliness soon passes, though, and the road
begins a steep climb toward Bohemia Mountain.

The country becomes more and more wild,
the road more and more steep, and the long drop
on your right will make you hug the center of the
road. Soon you may begin to notice "caves" dug
into the bank on the uphill side of the road.
These are mine shafts, some of which have been
sealed by heavy chains and iron-bar doors reminiscent of the jails in western movies.

As you carry on toward Bohemia City try to
imagine yourself walking out of these mountains
100 or so years ago, leading a mule loaded with
gold nuggets that you dug from deep inside
Bohemia Mountain.

If the snow stops you before you get to Bohemia City, resolve, as we did, to try again
some day when the conditions are more favorable.
The trip promises much adventure.

Go East

East of Eugene the Cascade Mountains rise
like a wall, shutting out the rest of the con-
tinent. The Cascades are a mountain-lover's
dream, a year-round playground for hikers, mountain climbers, fishermen, skiiers, campers,
geologists, rock climbers, hunters, and other
lovers of wild and isolated places.

There are two main routes to the east, out
of Eugene. Both are spectacular and both
follow rivers. The southern route, Highway 58,
follows the middle fork of the Willamette River
out of Eugene until just past Oakridge, where
the river and the road go their separate ways.
Sixty-seven miles from Eugene, Highway 58 enters central Oregon via the Willamette Pass.
The other road, Highway 126, follows the McKenzie
River into the Cascades, crossing into central
Oregon at either the McKenzie Pass or the
Santiam Pass, depending on the time of year and
the purpose of the trip.

A route that is slightly more spectacular than
the rest is Highway 242. It branches from the
McKenzie River Highway about five miles above
McKenzie Bridge. Closed much of the year by
snow, Highway 242 takes a steep scenic route
through lava fields across the McKenzie Pass
to Sisters. On a clear day, from the Dee Wright
Observatory on the very top of the Cascades, it
is possible to see all the Cascade snowpeaks from
Washington to California.

So many outstanding day trips are possible in
the Cascades that it is hard to isolate one as
more worthwhile than the others. The best thing
to do is to arm yourself with a Forest Service
Map (available from the headquarters of the Willamette National Forest, Federal Courthouse, in
Eugene, or from any of the Ranger District Stations

you pass along the way) and the gear appropriate
to your intended activity and seek whatever high-
mountain adventure strikes your fancy.

Though the Country is new, we have
no aristocracy and no high style of living.
Still we enjoy life as well as those
who roll in luxuries.

Eugene Skinner
to his sister
March 18, 1860

Cuisine, Haute and Not So Hot:

A Guide to Eating Out in Eugene

Cuisine, Haute and Not So Hot:
A Guide to Eating Out in Eugene

by
Mike Helm
and
Susan Porter

Restaurants in Eugene spring up like
mushrooms after a spring rain. They also,
occasionally, fold their tents and steal
away into the night, leaving only weather-
beaten signs and the shell of a building
where you might once have had a good meal.
More have opened than closed, though,
in recent years in Eugene and at last
count, not including the fast-food fran-
chises like MacDonald's, there were
more than 100 restaurants doing business
in Eugene.
The vast number of choices presupposes
the need for a guide to eating out in
Eugene, yet, until now, no guide existed.
Now the void is filled.
Everyone knows that there is more
than food involved in choosing a restaurant. The reviews that follow will
not only tell you whether you can get
a good meal, but will convey to you
something of the restaurant's character,
answer the question: What is this place
like?
To preserve our objectivity, we paid
for every meal, from the bagel soaked in
hot butter that ran all over my raincoat
in front of Zybach's Delicatessen, to
the Tournedo saute' Raphael eaten in
leisurely comfort at L'Auberge Du Vieux
Moulin. Restaurant managers were told
of the intended review only at the end
of the meal, in order to justify re-

quests for long-term loans of menus.

We are aware that restaurants disappear, that waitresses come and go, taking their particular temperament with them. We are aware that even the best chef can have an off day, that you, dear reader, may have had a rotten meal at a place we recommend, or that our experience may not have parallelled yours in some other way. Nevertheless, we were there, we ate, and this is what it was like.

Nasty Nora's Restaurant

3443 Hilyard
343-9582

No cards
No checks
No booze

"No Tar"
"No Mud"
"No Checks"
"Wipe Your Feet"
"Shirts and Shoes Required"
"Sorry, No Checks Accepted"
The rules are set down before you enter the building.
"Are you Nasty Nora?"
"Nope. I'm only her daughter, but I'm learnin'. Put that cup down and I'll pour you some coffee."
Tucked away in south Eugene between a gas

station and a neighborhood grocery store, screened
from the street by a few scraggly green shrubs,
and marked only by a wooden sign no larger than
the one that tells you "No Tar", is Nasty
Nora's Restaurant, the kind of place guidebook
writers dream of discovering. Workingmen
come here for inexpensive breakfasts or
lunches, and they go away with their bellies
full and change jingling in their jeans.

$1.60 at Nasty Nora's will get you two
eggs, hash browns, a thick slice of ham and
a couple of pieces of good buttered toast with
marmalade. Coffee costs 35¢, and a variety
of large omelettes, served with potatoes, go
for between $1.65 and $.90.

Saturdays are special at Nora's, as they serve
only breakfast until 11:00 or 12:00 or 1:00,
or whenever they run out of food. Then they
close for the weekend.

For a weekday lunch that's sure to cut down
on your consumption at dinner, try a cowburger.
It costs $1.60 and it'll fill your plate and
your stomach.

Little signs all over the place remind the
visitor to mind his or her manners. Nasty
Nora's is short on grace and subtlety, but long
on good food.

"No checks accepted ever." There it is again,
on the menu.

All right, all right. I'll pay cash, wipe
my feet, not spend too much time in the bathroom, keep my children in their chairs, get
up early on Saturday, not complain to the
cook, just eat my breakfast, cause no trouble,
and get out of here. The food's too good to
miss.

L'Auberge
Du Vieux Moulin
★ ★

770 W. 6th   Beer & Wine
485-8000   Visa, Mastercharge,
                              American Express
                              Reservations, please

It takes a far stretch of the imagination to
be transported in the course of one evening from
West 8th Street, where it roars through one of
Eugene's most beat-up neighborhoods, to the
quiet of a French countryside restaurant. At
L'Auberge Du Vieux Moulin you can make that
leap. Step inside this small old house, close
the door on the traffic noise, and you are in
France.

The menu is in French. French music washes
softly from the stereo. The restaurant's austere
decor and the quiet dignity of the hostess seem
appropriate to a special place. This is no
ordinary restaurant.

The menu at L'Auberge changes daily, depending
on what is available, fresh, at local markets.
Fish that has been frozen, for instance, is
never served at L'Auberge, because freezing
"alters the delicate flavor". Fish at L'Auberge
is either fresh or it is not on the menu. The
same policy applies to vegetables.

An average dinner at L'Auberge will cost around
$15.00, including a bottle of wine shared at the
table. A four course meal costs from $8.95,
for mignon de porc grand mere, to $12.75 for
scampi au cognac. The Tournedo saute Raphael,
a thick, tender filet mignon smothered in a savory demiglace sauce, is a delicious choice at
$10.50.

L'Auberge is the place to go when you plan to enjoy a leisurely dinner. Because of the care demanded by the classical French style of cooking, the service is slow and casual, and the meal, spiced with an excellent selection of wine and the company and conversation of good friends, deserves an entire evening of enjoyment.

The Union Oyster Bar

870 Pearl
686-2873

Beer & Wine
Mastercharge & Visa
Good checks accepted
with local i.d.

Why do people keep telling me this is a good place to eat?

The first time I ate at the Union Oyster Bar I ordered the clam strips. When they came I thought there had been a mistake.

"Nope," said the waitress. "Clam strips. Those are clam strips."

They weren't strips. They didn't taste like clams. They appeared to be crumbs of deep-fried batter, the kind that sometimes hang around in the grease after you've batter-fried fish or chicken. If there was an iota of clam in the entire pile of crumbs it escaped my attention. And I looked carefully.

The second time I ate at the Union Oyster Bar I ordered fish and chips. A limp lettuce salad, served on a little white China saucer with watery bleu cheese dressing, arrived first.

The main course looked good. Several large

pieces of fish, a big handful of French fries, and a round ball of Union Fry Bread crowded the plate. The fish and potatoes were golden brown.

Wait. The test is in the taste. The fish was mushy instead of flaky and tasted as though it had cooled and soaked in the same grease used to cook it.

Why do people keep telling me this is a good place to eat?

Eating successfully at the Union Oyster Bar is simply a matter of knowing what to order. Obviously, as I learned the hard way, no one should order from the "Fry Baskets" section of the menu.

The Union Oyster Bar is a comfortable, slightly classy place where soup lovers gather. Order gumbo or shrimp and cheddar soup and you'll walk away singing. Seafood salads and appetizers are delicious and large enough to fill a big eater. Bagels 'n' things from the sandwich selection is a Humble bagel and cream cheese served with a generous helping of lox, shrimp, or crab.

Lunch at the Union Oyster Bar can cost as little as $1.15 for a small bowl of soup, a ball of Union Fry Bread, and a few chunks of fruit, to $4.95 for a large bowl of gumbo or oyster stew or a steak sandwich.

Whatever you do, don't order anything fried at the Union Oyster Bar.

La Primavera

388 W. 7th   Full Bar
485-0601   Checks okay with i.d.
                  Visa, Mastercharge
                  American Express

"So glad you're with us tonight," is your greeting at the door to La Primavera.

You <u>are</u> glad to be there. You have just walked down a European garden path of manicured little green trees and soft muted lights, onto the expansive front porch of an impeccably restored older home.

You peek in the window, sample the atmosphere in advance: white tablecloths, white candles, individually rolled napkins, original oil paintings, shining crystal, flowers. A curved oak staircase gracefully spirals up to a second floor where there is additional seating and a small cocktail lounge peacefully furnished with couches and chairs, like an elegant sitting room in a castle.

"Hello. My name is Jeffrey, your waiter tonight."

You are handed an elaborate wine list, and a menu printed on one large sheet of parchment paper. The name of the Chef de Cuisine (Ray Sewell) is printed at the bottom.

It is obvious that Jeffrey is an experienced waiter, that he has tasted the food. He is most helpful in describing in an unpretentious manner the innumerable specialties of veal, poultry, beef tenderloin, lamb, fish, and pasta. He will remain attentive but not obtrusive throughout the evening.

A dinner at La Primavera, including homemade soup, salad, and delicious French bread, costs from $8.00 to $45.00. Forty dollars will buy a fresh rack of Willamette lamb garni or Chateaubriand Sauce Vin Blanc. Count on spending at least $15 to $20 per person (conservative estimate) for dinner, wine, coffee, and dessert, more if you go flambe with desserts or want appetizers.

Whatever you order--a superb cut of beef, filet of sole, frog legs, sweetbreads, chicken livers, or quail--you will get just what you pay for:

La Primavera

outstanding food, carefully seasoned with fresh
herbs, and topped with marvelous sauces and
marinades.

The intermingling of flavors in the sauces reminds you that your cook is a master, trained some-
where other than in Eugene. Sometimes the
sauces are so flavorful that you can lose sight
and taste of the essential flavor of the meat
or fish underneath.

The desserts are outstanding and very rich,
but well worth the investment if you have the time,
money, and room in your stomach. A dessert tray
with an assortment of incredible in-house pastries
($2.25 each) will tempt you. There are several
special desserts for two, like Crepes Suzette
with fresh fruits and nuts in Creme Anglaise,
Cherries Jubilee, Spanish Coffee, and Souffle
au Chocalat Ghirardelli.

La Primavera also has an extensive lunch
menu, featuring salads, soup, sandwiches, omelettes, pastas, seafood, and beef. Lunch prices
are from $5.00 to $8.00.

An eating establishment that charges high
prices should deliver food, service, and atmosphere on an equally lofty plane. La Primavera
delivers. Try it.

Aunt Hattie's Restaurant

400 Blair Boulevard   No cards
485-0152   No booze
                       Checks okay with i.d.

This old white wooden building at the corner
of 4th and Blair is the sort of place where

Little Red Ridinghood's grandmother might have lain in bed awaiting a visit from the wolf. Wood frame windows look out upon a generous expanse of green grass and a few large trees, a buffer between Aunt Hatty's and the maddening rush of traffic that rackets by on Blair Boulevard. Aunt Hatty's is the kind of place a reviewer <u>wants</u> to be good.

Well, the waitress is attractive and friendly, and the menu doesn't look bad.

The most expensive meal is only $2.95, a main course of hot roast beef, chicken fried steak or breaded veal, served with mashed potatoes and gravy, salad, vegetables, and rolls. The most expensive breakfast, served all day, is steak and eggs for $2.50. The menu offers a good lunch, too, and change back from your $2.00.

However, at Aunt Hatty's you get what you pay for, maybe less. The grilled ham and cheese sandwich, for example, is burned on the outside and barely warm on the inside. Aunt Hatty's hamburgers are cooked until they are black and dry. Sandwiches and hamburgers are served quickly, accompanied by a tiny packet of potato chips that is almost impossible to open.

The Vegetarian Restaurant

270 W. 8th   No booze
342-4335

The Vegetarian Restaurant is an immaculate, highly-ordered eating establishment, conceived by the Seventh Day Adventist Church and located in the old Porter's Foods Unlimited Store. It serves--what else?--good vegetarian food at reasonable prices.

An entree of creamed chow mein, a side of peas, a glass of milk, and a homemade date bar costs $2.05. Ninety-cent entrees include garbanzo potpourri, mushroom noodle casserole, tamale pie, lentil or cottage cheese loaf, and stroganoff.

The standing buffet menu includes an excellent borsht soup with sour cream (60¢/cup, 95¢/bowl), a green salad bar (95¢ or $2.50), fruit salad with orange yogurt dressing ($1.25), or a selection of three sandwiches. Take particular care not to choose vegetables that are overcooked.

A particularly good buy is the Unburger (95¢, $1.10 with cheese), a tasty soy patty on a wholewheat bun, accompanied by good tomato sauce and an attractive garnish of tomato, lettuce, onion, carrots, and olives.

Drinks include a selection of natural fruit juices, milk, herb teas, and a coffee substitute. Carrot juice is squeezed fresh to your order.

To enjoy the Vegetarian Restaurant, you must be in the mood to eat cafeteria-style meals with no meat products, no alcohol, no coffee, and no particular environmental pizzaz.

If you are looking for a quiet, un-flourescent, absolutely smoke-free downtown place to be alone with a good book when every other place is convulsed in the throes of lunch hour rush, or if you are looking for a quiet place to talk with a friend with no intrusion from surrounding chatter and clatter, the Vegetarian may be for you.

The Wild Plum

✶ ✶

1081 Valley River Way
484-2666　　　　Mastercharge & Visa
　　　　　　　　No booze
　　　　　　　　Local checks with i.d.

The Wild Plum is just an average American
eatery, a nice Denny's or Sambo's, but, for
the shopper stranded in the wasteland of Valley River Center's vast lunchtime desert, the
food here is worth the walk across the parking
lot and the dodge through the traffic on Valley
River Way.

The Wild Plum's most expensive entre is a
New York steak dinner for $6.45.

The soup of the day, clam chowder on Friday,
is served by the ladle. Ninety-five cents
gets you one small ladle, $1.65 gets you two,
plus a large chunk of light and fluffy corn-
bread served with whipped honey and butter.
This, for the small and moderate appetite,
is the best bargain on the menu.

Sandwiches and hamburgers go for from
$1.95 to $3.65, and there is a special
section of the menu for children.

Twenty-nine kinds of pie "made here and
baked daily", are listed on the back of the
menu. A slice of pie costs from 85¢ to
$1.15. While not exactly like "home made"
pie, Wild Plum pie is better than pie
usually offered in similar places. Whole
pies are also available. "You'll be plum welcome
when you take a pie home," the menu reminds
us.

The service at the Wild Plum is friendly
and easy-going. Diners sit in oaken booths
on wild plum vinyl upholstery. The vaulted
ceiling and walls are Douglas fir, stained

to match the oak booths and window frames.
An impressive collection of antiques and artwork
by Oregon craftsmen complements the design
scheme.

If you're looking for lunch at Valley
River Center, you'll get more for your money
and you'll get it more comfortably at the
Wild Plum.

🙂🗿🗿🗿🗿🗿🗿🗿🗿🗿🗿🗿🗿🗿🗿🗿🗿🗿🗿🗿🗿🗿🗿🗿

The Treehouse
Restaurant

✶ ✶

1769 Franklin Boulevard
485-3444   Full bar
                            Visa and Mastercharge
                            Local checks with
                            bank i.d.

The Treehouse Restaurant of the Greentree
Motel is an informal and elegant window on
Franklin Boulevard. The service here is su-
perb and the food is excellent.

Diners are seated on wicker furniture in an
indoor patio, surrounded by green plants and
bathed in soft music and natural light. Tables
are dressed in white linen and decorated with
a perfectly-pleated napkin fan and a small vase
of daisies or a single red rose.

The Treehouse is a good place to talk with
a good friend, to feel special without having
to dress up. It's a marvelous place to be
gentle with yourself in midafternoon on a
weekday over a delicious French layered Ni-
coise salad with a choice of tuna or Oregon

114

shrimp ($3.25-$4.25) and your own quarter litre carafe of crisp white wine ($1.35)

The luncheon menu includes sandwiches served with a choice of delicious homemade soup or salad ($3.25-$3.75), whole-meal salads carefully arranged like a still-life painting, chicken breasts with soup or salad ($3.50) or the Treehouse special of soup and salad $2.95).

All food is served quickly, by quietly attentive waiters and waitresses.

Full dinners, including soup or salad and the vegetable of the day, range from $6.95 to $8.95. Treehouse features beef stroganoff, five seafood dishes, lamb ribs, and marinated chicken or chicken curry mandarin. Children's portions are available on request.

A small, tasteful selection of domestic and imported still and sparkling wines and beers is available. Cocktails are served at your table, or in a small, dark lounge that is too much in contrast to the light and airy dining room.

A selection of tempting desserts on a rolling dessert tray ($1.50 each) and a cup of rich, aromatic coffee can top off your meal at the Treehouse.

Collier House

* *

1170 E. 13th   No booze
686-5286   No cards
                      Checks okay with i.d.

This gracious old house has presided over many changes on the University of Oregon campus since it was built by physics professor George Collier in 1885.

Originally, it stood on a 9-acre piece of
property that stretched up University Street to
where the Pioneer Cemetery is today. Hendricks
Hall now stands in George Collier's cherry orchard, and, until the University acquired the
building and property for $5000 in 1895, there
was no University property on the south side
of 13th Street. Collier's neighbors, the
McMurrys, lived across University Street in a
2-story white frame house in the center of
what is now the Erb Memorial Union. Thirteenth
Street was an unpaved track delineated by
a white rail fence.

Collier was fired by the University in
1895, and the house became home to University
of Oregon presidents from that time until
the 1930's. The last University president to
live in the Collier House was Donald Erb, for
whom the Erb Memorial Union is named.

The Faculty Club was given use of the
building in the 1940's. It remained,
until 1972, the exclusive domain of Faculty
Club members, but, because of a budget defi-
cit, it was then opened to University staff
members and students. Now it is open weekdays
for lunch, from 11:30 to 2:00, to the general
public.

The menu is a fairly average sandwich-soup-
salad lunch menu. The difference is in the pre-
paration and the price. The items are inexpensive and well-prepared. The Reuben, for
instance, costs $2.00, and does not appear to
have been slapped together and dipped in grease
before it hit the plate. It is warm, the cheese
melted, and the bread is fresh but not soggy.
Even the lowly hamburger, for $1.35, appears to
have been prepared with care. What's more, it
tastes good. The service is quick, careful,
and cheerful.

Though the elegance of the old house has been
remodeled out of the main downstairs dining areas,
it is still easy to experience something of

116

George Collier's regal style in the rest of the house. The long walkway through the grass from 13th Street, the imposing facade of the old house, the high ceilings, large rooms and wide hallways, graceful sitting rooms where University presidents once took their leisure, and the view from the little balcony atop the front porch are all still there, awaiting the appreciation of the lunch-time visitor.

The Trawler

* *

11 East Park
484-5730

Mastercharge, Visa
Full Bar
No cigar smoking,
please.

The Trawler is the place in Eugene for seafood. In fact, the Trawler is one of the places in Eugene where atmosphere, fine, friendly service, and excellent food combine to make dining a special experience.

Located in the basement of the South Park Building, the Trawler is accessible to wheel-chair-bound individuals via the elevator from the sidewalk level.

Large photographs of deep-sea fishing action abound on the walls of the Trawler's bar and dining areas. They catch the mood of the sea and project a kind of restless excitement into the fantasies of the viewer.

Dinner prices start at $6.50, for grilled oysters or Pacific fish casserole, and soar to $15.95 for Australian lobster tails or $17.00 for lobster and tenderloin. Pacific razor clams, "lightly breaded and quickly fried to a golden brown", are a delicious choice for $7.75. The

seafood quiche, for $7.50, is a quarter of a pie.
The crust is just as advertised, flaky, and the
filling is a rich, savory mixture of crab and
shrimp, bacon, onions, mushrooms, and cheese.

A word about the bread. All dinners at the
Trawler come with bread and butter. If you are
a devotee of good bread, you must have dinner
at the Trawler. The bread is hot and fresh.
The butter melts on contact, the crust is
crisp and chewy, and your waitress will keep
bringing it until you've had enough.

Attendants at the Trawler are friendly, know-
ledgable, and opinionated. "I wouldn't have
that. The mushrooms are a much better deal."
They are efficient but not pushy, and they go
out of their way to make each diner feel welcome.

In every way, a Trawler dinner is one of
the best meals you'll get in Eugene.

The Spindle Cafe

395 W. 5th   No booze
342-2075   No cards
                    Local checks okay
                    with i.d.

"I've been reading so much about the bad
effects of smoking, drinking, and overeating
that I finally decided to give up reading."
          Sign on the wall in the Spindle Cafe

The Spindle Cafe is a down-home, store-front
cafe run by Bill and Lois, who specialize in
good breakfasts and lunches. Nearly 50 personal
coffee mugs hang on the wall in the Spindle,
silently testifying that this is a place with
a large repeat trade. A small pink building

with a bright blue door, the Spindle gets its
name from two long, knobby chair spindles
attached to the door.

Bill is the cook, Lois the waitress. The
atmosphere in the Spindle is 1950 linoleum, for-
mica, and plastic seat covers with shiny metal
rivets on the back. You can hear the bacon
sizzle on the grill, just behind the knotty
pine wall that separates the eating area from
the tiny kitchen.

Breakfast is served until 11 a.m. Bacon or
sausage and egg, hashbrowns, and toast costs
$2.40. The serving is ample and the hashbrowns
are tasty and crisp, even if they are not homemade. Omelettes range from $1.75 to $2.40.
Hashbrowns and toast are included in that
price.

The lunch menu features nine kinds of hamburgers, ranging in price from $1.50 to $2.10.
A Spindle Burger, double beef pattie with double
cheese on a toasted bun, costs $1.75, or $2.30
with French fries. Sandwiches include a triple
decker club sandwich with ham, turkey, and
bacon on toast with lettuce and tomato for
$2.00.

Home made soup cooks all morning in a large
stock pot. It is available for lunch for 45¢
and 75¢ a bowl.

The Refectory

2000 Centennial Boulevard
342-5231   Full Bar
                      Mastercharge, Visa
                      American Express

Okay, salad lovers, here's your place.

The Refectory salad bar is magnificent. It is a long stainless steel cabinet filled with large bowls of crisp lettuce, juicy little tomatoes, beans, sprouts, croutons that don't taste like presto-log, rich dressings, and bacon bits. What's more, you can go back again and again, though, if you stack it right, once by the salad bar is enough.

The rest of the menu is average American restaurant, as is the preparat'on, but once you've been by the salad bar it won't make any difference.

Dinner at The Refectory, after the mandatory hour or so wait in the bar for your table, will probably cost around $12.00 per person, including the before-dinner drink and a bottle of wine with dinner. Entrees run from $5.75 for the Mahi Mahi to $11.95 for steak and lobster. The Refectory Cut of prime rib, at $8.75, is the specialty of the house.

Stay away from the fish, especially if it's scampi. "A changing selection," the menu says. "Your waiter will be glad to tell you about it." He did. Scampi, simmered in a sauce with vegetables. Sounded good. The sauce looked like canned custard, but was thinner, like Elmer's Glue. With the scampi, it tasted as though it had all been simmered together by the Purina Company and brought to the Refectory in a bag.

The Refectory has an excellent wine selection, friendly and--with the possible exception of the young man who recommended the fish--knowledge-able waiters and waitresses.

If you like salad, if you choose wisely from the menu, if you enjoy a lengthy barside wait for a table, you will find an evening at The Refectory an enjoyable experience.

The Excelsior

✶ ✶

754 E. 13th   Full Bar
342-6963   Mastercharge,
15% service charge   Visa, American
in lieu of tip for   Express
parties of 6 or more   Checks okay with
                               bank guarantee card

It is probable that if a Eugene restaurant
has a superstar chef or baker, he or she once
worked at the Excelsior. Poppi's, Biederbeck's,
the Metropol, the Trawler, and, undoubtedly
some of the others, all owe something of what
is best about them to the restaurant that has
become a sort of Godfather to fine dining in
Eugene, the Excelsior.

When it opened in 1972, the Excelsior oc-
cupied only half of the downstairs of a fine
old fraternity house on 13th Street, but it
expanded in a short time to include the entire floor. In fine weather meals were served
in the open air on the expansive porch that
hugged the building on the front and around
the side. An ill-conceived remodelling project
a few years ago obscured the genteel architectural flavor of the building from the outside,
but the grace and style of the old place is
still discernable once inside, and it complements perfectly the friendly, stylish service and good French food that have become the
hallmark of the Excelsior Cafe.

Dining at the Excelsior is never cheap, but
a good meal may be put together from any one of
three menus without bankrupting most people.
Beggar's Banquet, a $3.25 lunchtime favorite,
is a large bowl of the soup of the day, cheese,
fruit and French bread. Excelsior French bread
is the best. Anywhere. Salads, sandwiches,
quiche, and casserole are also offered on the

lunch menu, ranging in price from $1.50 to $4.00.

Dinners include soup, salad, vegetables, and French bread, and they cost from $6.50 to $11.00. Sausage and apple pie is a generous wedge of pork sausage, apples, onions, and herbs, baked in a pie crust. Try it or the chicken, Supreme de Volaille Madere, chicken breast cooked to juicy perfection, sauteed in butter and served in a creamy wine sauce. Dessert freaks have been known to collapse in frustration as they tried to choose just one of the offerings from the Excelsior dessert tray.

For a special treat on any Sunday, try a Sunday champagne brunch at the Excelsior. A glass of bubbly for $1.35, Omelette Grandmere for $2.75, and your Sunday is off to a lovely, lazy start.

Any meal at the Excelsior is a special treat, to be lingered over and savored like a glass of fine wine.

The Homefried Truckstop

790 East 14th   No cards
344-9988   No booze
               No checks

The Homefried Truckstop, a restaurant run by a collective of "about 30 people" in an old fraternity house a couple of blocks from the University of Oregon campus, serves up good, economical meals, and good, down home music, all day, every day.

"We try to maintain a balance between serving good, wholesome food to the community and making a living for ourselves. We hope you enjoy being here..." says the blurb on the menu. Judging from its continued existence and the reasonable prices charged for hefty servings, the Truckstop is succeeding.

The menu is biased toward vegetarian meals, though meat is available at a price. For instance, $1.45 will buy you a breakfast of two eggs, "homefries"--large chunks of real potatoes, fried with the skin still on--and two thick slices of homemade bread. Add one slice of bacon and you've added 50¢ to the tab. A slice of ham costs $1.35.

Lunch runs from $1.00, for a basic peanut butter and jelly sandwich, to $3.40 for a ham and Swiss cheese sandwich. Salads go for $1.45 to $2.65.

If a soyburger is your idea of a good dinner, you can get one at the Truckstop for $2.10. The most expensive dinner on the menu is the fish dinner for $4.40.

Music adds an extra dimension to meals at the Truckstop. Performers are scheduled approximately a month in advance, and at the first of each month the Truckstop publishes a calendar that tells who will perform on each day.

The crowd, mostly casual campus-types and a few senior citizens who drop by to take advantage of the 10% discount offered them by the Truckstop, can sip coffee in the morning to the rhythm of a piano-guitar duet, and then come back for a soyburger dinner to the sound of some old-time fiddling.

If you like reasonably priced good food and good folksy music in warm friendly surroundings, you can find it all at the Homefried Truckstop.

Woolworth's
Harvest House

✱ ✱

930 Willamette   No booze
344-1012   All major credit
Local checks okay   cards
with i.d.

"Anniversary Special. SAVE. SAVE. America's Special Burger with Cheese with Large Coke $1.67. Roast Beef Dinner $1.75."

Come to the Harvest House, located across from the shampoo section, next to the jewelry counter, a few feet away from a crying kid and a cash register. The sounds--hot oil sizzling for a basket of fries, a grill being scraped for a grilled tuna san, the grape and orange drink bubbler machines--tell you this is the place.

Eating at Woolworth's is a way back to the 50's, when a five-and-dime store luncheonette was the neighborhood meeting place.

The food is cheap and good (though sometimes a little overcooked and greasy), the portions ample, the atmosphere predictably folksy, and the service fast and friendly. You may not see your own best friends here, but you will see a cross-section of America, particularly the young who a-dore French fries and a large coke, the pie and coffee breakers, and the person who likes a robust roast turkey dinner at lunch time.

You'll be fascinated by the number of handy-dandy kitchen machines along the 20-foot counter (from bun warmers to milkshake machines), by the large shiny convenience centers stacked with hundreds of premeasured precut hamburger patties on waxed paper, and by the three intercoms with

red blinking lights placed along the counter
for calling in orders.

A "1+1+1 Breakfast" (one egg, one slice
bacon, one slice buttered toast and jelly) costs
$1.25. You can be extravagant and get two eggs
with ham, toast, and hashbrowns for $2.10. Table
and chair seating faces the mall—not a bad place
to watch the workday begin if you are not bothered
by cigarette smoke.

A turkey sandwich with beverage for lunch will
set you back $2.60. A hamburger platter with fries
costs $1.80, a tuna fish salad plate $1.99,
soup and sandwich combinations cost $1.89, and
a shrimp basket with fries and a roll costs
$2.29. A large bowl of soup costs only 65¢.

For faster service, you are asked to order
by number from the menu.

"Let's see. I'll take a 69B." That's a
grilled cheese with tomato for $1.25.

Pietro's
Gold Coast
Pizza Parlor

4006 Franklin Boulevard
746-8245   Beer & Wine
                No cards
                Local checks okay
                with i.d.

At Pietro's, pizza is an afterthought.
First are the lights, the brash blare of
"PIZZA!" at motorists on Franklin Boulevard, the

promise of esoteric adventure to insects up from the Willamette.

Then the train. Who wouldn't like to ride through the summer evening in their own open-air car on a tiny railroad?

Inside, once you've dragged your children from the train--after all, we came here to eat--confusion reigns. Little children scamper everywhere underfoot. Adolescents challenge machines in a tiny doorway arcade, and fat ladies in black polyester pants shoulder through the crowd on the way to the bathroom.

Were the Gay 90's really like this?

Tables and chairs are strewn across an acre of floorspace, surrounded by several hundred yards of garish whorehouse wallpaper, white enameled woodwork, large windows and, out there, a merry-go-round.

"Can I, Daddy? Can I? Can I?"

The menu lists 26 varieties of pizza, ranging in price from a small plain pizza ("Pietro's special cheese blend") for $2.50 to a giant Pizza Maker's Special ("A Deli of a Pizza") for $10.80. "Your choice of pizza is not limited to the above combination of ingredients. Extra charge for extras. Half 'n half pizzas are at the price of the higher half. We wuz glad to do it...Pietro."

Order. Sit down with a beer. "$2.00 Pitcher 50¢," says the sign. That reads like a bargain, but it isn't. Take a window seat and you can watch the river roll by and keep an eye on your kids as they wear out the merry-go-round. Pietro's even has a non-smoker's section.

When your number's called, collect the pizza from the counter, signal the kids to dismount, and no one even notices that the Hula Loola is soggy in the middle and burnt on the edges, or that it sports only an occasional lump of pineapple and (How'd they do this?) it's only barely warm.

Don't forget to pick up your free balloon on a stick on the way out.

鿃鿃鿃鿃鿃鿃鿃鿃鿃鿃鿃鿃鿃鿃鿃鿃鿃鿃鿃鿃鿃鿃

Seymour's Greenery Restaurant

* *

999 Willamette
344-4022

No bar, but booze is available
Mastercharge, Visa, American Express, Diner's Club

The French fries at Seymour's don't seem to be made from potatoes. It occurred to me as one melted in my mouth—I didn't even chew—that they were probably squeezed from a tube, like toothpaste.

Seymour's looks better than it is. It is the proverbial clean, well-lighted place, highlighted by dramatic open-beam architecture, and an expanse of windows through which you can watch the mall rats and the LTD buses as they interact at 10th and Willamette. It is comfortable, conveniently located on the downtown mall, and the waitresses are friendly and efficient. The only thing it does not have is fine food.

Lunch will set you back from 55¢, for a bowl of the soup of the day, to $4.25 for a sirloin steak sandwich. The specialty of the house is

"The Greenery's Own Finger Steak" for $3.95.
The Reuben, for $2.50, is a "sandwich to re-
member", as the menu promises. You'll remember it as it lies heavily in the pit of
your stomach. The Pastrami, for $2.25, is a
smaller than average portion of pastrami
clamped between two soggy slices of dark rye
bread.

All the sandwiches come with your choice of
salad or French fries. The salad is a small
handful of limp lettuce on a tiny white plate.
The French fries appear to have come from a
tube and will melt in your mouth. It's a toss-
up, but, given that choice again, I'd choose
neither.

回回回回回回回回回回回回回回回回回回回回回回回回

East Broadway

Pizzeria

* * * * * * * * * * * * * * * * * * * *

652 E. Broadway   Beer & Wine
345-4114   Visa & Mastercharge
                         Checks okay with
                         bank i.d.

The East Broadway Pizzeria has the pizzeria
basics: low lights, vigrant colors, small and
large tables and booths, lots of people and a
sense of revelry. What it lacks are candles on
the table--so you can see who you are eating
with, and appreciate the Chicago-style wall
decor--decent background music, and a non-
smoking section.

The atmosphere, then, is average, as is
the service. The pizza, however, is superb.

The specialty at the East Broadway Pizzeria

is good, thick, Chicago-style pizza, with a
Northside or a Southside option.

Northside pizza is baked in a pan. It
comes with a mild tomato sauce over the top, and
is so thick that it takes about a half hour to
cook. Northside costs from 50¢ to $1.00
more than the Southside.

Southside pizza is spicier. It has cheese
on top, a thinner crust, and is baked free-
form on brick. The basic Southside cheese pizza
comes in three sizes ($2.70, $4.15, $5.55) plus
a create-your-own pizza with twelve possible
ingredients at 30¢ to 50¢ each.

A large Southside pizza with Canadian bacon,
mushrooms, onions, and sliced tomatoes costs
$7.55. The same Northside pizza costs $1.00
more. Not a bad price for a great pizza.

While you wait for your pizza, try a basket
of hot garlic bread with cheese, or a green
salad with tomatoes, either for 75¢. They
are tasty choices with wine or beer.

Accuardi's
Old Town
Pizza Company

174 E. Broadway
342-3366

No cards
Beer & Wine
Checks okay with i.d.

At Accuardi's, pizza comes steaming to your
old oaken dining table on a tray carried by a

smiling waitress.

Tall floor lamps, crowned by silk lampshades with long fringes, filter soft rays through cigarette smoke and pizza fumes, bathing pepperoni, pineapple, cheese, and beer in a hazy antique luxuriance. Nearby, in a dining area that looks like your great grandmother's parlor, diners are swallowed up by fat old chairs, bulging comfortably around a beat-up coffee table. The theme is old and comfortable clutter, complemented successfully by woven bird cages, oak kitchen queens, ornate oak high chairs, plants, machinery, posters, and the brick walls and fir floor of this old warehouse.

The menu offers two sizes of pizza, basic small at $2.00 and basic large at $3.75, and eleven of the usual additions, from capocolla to pineapple, at 65¢ each. Two large pizzas ("serves two", the menu says) are sufficient for our family of four small children and two adults, with enough left over, usually, for the kids' lunches the following day.

The large pizza is a much better buy than the small pizza, which is invariably long on crust and short on everything else. The large pizza is the best in Eugene, with a thick, bready crust that's assertive and chewy, but doesn't dwarf the generous, tasty filling.

Long-bladed fans cut lazy circles in the smoke over the massive oak and mirror bar where you can watch yourself order beer. A not-quite-full 42 ounce pitcher costs $2.25 and they'll top it off if you ask, but not without a grimace. Milk, wine, and soft drinks are also available.

The clientele here is decidedly mixed. Anyone--your kid's ESP soccer coach, or a guy in beads, beard and bearskin who looks a little too much like Charles Manson, or the weird professor who put his hand on your leg in his office that time, or your brother-in-law's psychiatrist-- might be sitting in antique-y comfort at the next oaken table.

The atmosphere is comfortable and interesting, the waitresses cheerful, the food good. As a bonus, Accuardi's even has clean johns--the kind where kids can go by themselves and not come back with some hideous disease.

Accuardi's Old Town Pizza Company is a good place to eat.

⌐⌐⌐⌐⌐⌐⌐⌐⌐⌐⌐⌐⌐⌐⌐⌐⌐⌐⌐⌐⌐⌐⌐⌐⌐⌐⌐⌐

El Sombrero
* *

146 E. 11th
344-6634

Mastercharge, Visa
No checks
Beer

If you're looking for good Mexican food at a reasonable price, El Sombrero is for you.

Eating at El Sombrero is like eating in a small, hectic cafeteria. Everyone eats in one room. It is lined on the sides with plastic-clad booths and jammed in the middle with rickety-looking wooden tables.

The average diner will spend between $4.00 and $5.00, which includes the price of a bottle of beer and a small basket of corn tortilla chips. I always order portions separately from the a la carte section of the menu, as I enjoy the added flexibility, and the rice and tea that come with the dinner order don't seem to justify the extra expense.

One enchilada or burrito, which comes with refried beans even when ordered a la carte, is an entire dinner for a smaller child, and a delicious selection for an adult who is putting together his or her own combination.

At dinner time El Sombrero is jammed. Over-worked waitresses scurry out of the small kitchen, loaded with hot plates of steaming tacos, tamales, enchiladas and tostadas, then hustle back to clatter load after load of dirty dishes onto the too-small counter near the kitchen entryway. There is, in such crowded and busy quarters, an ever-present danger that someone's dinner will be spilled on your head, but no one's ever is, and the waitresses hurry about their business in a cheerful, friendly, and efficient manner.

If you like Mexican food and you're not too fussy about quiet or exotic surroundings, you'll like El Sombrero.

Nice Cream Parlor

325 Blair Boulevard
687-0391   No booze

"When you next dig into a luscious-looking ice cream sundae, think of it as a conglomeration of paint remover, leather cleaner, antifreeze, lice killer and coal tar...and THINK TWICE!"

With this, the Nice Cream Parlor lets it be known that their ice cream is made the old-fashioned way, with rock salt and ice, real milk products, real fruits, and all natural flavoring ingredients.

The result is delicious and unusual, but all this real-ness is expensive. Nice cream comes by the scoop--50¢ for a single, 95¢ for a double, or, the ultimate, $1.35 for a triple.

If you dream of chocolate, try the Brown
Death Special. It sells for $1.60 and consists
of layers of chocolate cake, chocolate ice cream,
chocolate sauce, and chocolate sprinkles.

The Nice Cream Parlor perches like an old barn
on Blair island, between traffic lanes. It is an
old country homestead, with a full porch, a
fireplace room, lots of windows, and a little
grass out front. I can't help but wonder what
the house was like before streets and commercial
interests infiltrated the neighborhood. The
noise of the traffic does not invade the house,
so cars remain something to look at between bites.

The Nice Cream Parlor serves much more than
ice cream. There is a spaghetti feast (all you
can eat for $3.25) with live music every Thursday
from 6-9 p.m. An excellent lunch for $2.00 or
less is served daily. Specials include soup,
salads, and sandwiches.

Hearty homemade soup with French bread costs
85¢ or $1.15, a melted cheese, mushroom, tomato
and sprout sandwich is $1.80, and a daily special
of a tostado with chicken and avocado goes for
$2.00. A super salad costs $2.50. It is very
large, and consists of a double portion of tossed
salad with avocado and cheese.

Beverages are simple and to the point--coffee,
tea, milk, or juice.

If you can ignore unshined floors, unsightly
woodwork, unsparkling windows, and a bulletin-
board type entryway, you'll be able to relax
and enjoy the charm of this un-plastic eating
establishment, and maybe even bask in the sun
with a friend for a long chat.

Coffee and Donuts

* *

Kt's Bakery and Sandwich Shoppe
955 Overpark Arcade   Area for nonsmokers
343-6616

At KT's, for no extra charge, a friendly waitress will slide whatever pastry you choose to
accompany your coffee through a microwave oven
and bring it to your table hot, with a chunk of
butter melting on top and running down the
sides. More a coffee shop than a bakery, KT's
is a nice place to stop and rest while shopping
in downtown Eugene.

The Donut Express
5th Street Public Market
485-4554

Sugar-coated lumps of heavy dough are the
specialty here. Like gobs of lead, they'll
sit in your belly for hours after consumption,
defying all efforts to dissolve them. If you
eat one of these horrors on your mid-morning
coffee break, you'll come to your dinner table
still heavy from the experience. When you're
looking for a snack in the 5th Street Public
Market and your eyes light on the Donut Express,
keep looking.

The Metropol and Coffee Corner
5th Street Public Market
296 E. 5th

The magic combination at the 5th Street Public
Market is a croissant, fresh and crisp, with
a big gob of butter and a generous helping of
jam from the Metropol, complemented by a cup of

hot fresh coffee, available weak, medium, or strong, from the Coffee Corner.

The Giant Grinder
1485 East 19th
342-6767

If fresh cinnamon rolls and plenty of hot, fresh coffee with no charge for refills appeals to you, this is a worthwhile midmorning stopping place.

Darby's Donuts
Valley River Center
342-8241

Darby's Donuts is part of Valley River Center's World's Fare Restaurant complex. In addition to Darby's, the complex includes the Soup Kettle, the Ranch Hand, and Gulliver's Grog 'n' Galley. Darby's coffee is good and refills are free. The donuts are light and fresh. Here you can sit on the edge of the mall, dunk a donut, sip coffee, and watch the rest of the world hurry by. Darby's is an ideal place for a mid-morning break.

The Rolling Pin Bakery & Coffee Shop
645½ River Road
688-7201

The freshest thing in the Rolling Pin Bakery, on a rainy Monday morning last February, was a wrinkled, coffee-stained Oregonian someone left on the counter. The Rolling Pin seems to specialize in watery coffee and old pastry. Don't try it.

Dave's Pie Shop
1331 Willamette
345-3143

Primarily a pie shop, the fact that it looks
like a coffee shop is apparently an accident.
The coffee is watery and the pastry choice is
practically nonexistent. For a mid-morning
pick-me-up, this is not the place. Wait till
later in the day and try the pie.

◨◨◨◨◨◨◨◨◨◨◨◨◨◨◨◨◨◨◨◨◨◨◨◨◨◨◨◨

Of Dogs

and

One Delicatessen

✱ ✱

Jeb's Good Dogs
1350 Alder
686-2931

Jeb's Good Dogs is a hole in the wall next
to the Pegasus Bookstore. Put an order and some
money into the hole and you will receive either
Eugene's second best hot dog or a better than
average hamburger. You can put your elbows
on the planks Jeb has set up as tables on the
porch outside his tiny kitchen, munch your hot
dog, and watch the rain spattering down on
Alder Street.

Giant Grinder Delicatessen
2165 West 11th, 484-4040
1485 East 19th, 342-6767
1677 Coburg Road, 342-2050

   If you haven't eaten a Grinder since their
bad old days of surly service and crumbly, fall-
apart bread, it's time to give them another try.
The new Grinders, served in fresh chewy bread
from the Giant Grinder's own bakery, are superb,
and one is enough for two hungry people. The
service is fast and friendly and, with three
locations, they are within quick reach of any
part of Eugene. Giant Grinders are a good lunch,
and, at least at their East 19th location, a
good place to stop for mid-morning coffee and a
fresh cinnamon roll.

Frank E. Furter
5th Street Public Market
296 E. 5th

   Absolutely the best hot dog in Eugene. A dollar and a quarter buys a fat, juicy frank and
all the relish, onions, mustard and ketchup
you'll ever need in a bun that doesn't fall apart
when you pick it up.

▨▨▨▨▨▨▨▨▨▨▨▨▨▨▨▨▨▨▨▨▨▨▨▨▨▨

Saturday Night in Eugene

Naming Your Poison;
A Guide to Drinking in Eugene

Booze in Oregon

· ·

The sale of alcoholic beverages in Oregon is regulated by the Oregon Liquor Control Commission (OLCC). The OLCC issues four kinds of liquor licenses, two of which allow the establishment to sell hard liquor and two that do not.

Most taverns in Oregon hold Retail Malt Beverage Licenses, allowing them to sell malt beverages with an alcohol content of not more than 8% by weight, and wines with an alcohol content of not more than 14% by weight, for consumption on the premises, or in the bottle for off-premise consumption. Retail Malt Beverage Licenses go to establishments whose principal business activity is the sale of beverages, but who may also sell food.

A restaurant with a Malt Beverage License can sell, for consumption on the premises only, malt beverages with an alcohol content of not more than 8% by weight, and wine with an alcohol content of not more than 21% by weight. Restaurant Malt Beverage Licenses are granted to establishments whose principal business activity is the sale of food--pizza parlors and fish and chips restaurants, for example.

For hard liquor you must go to an establishment with a Dispenser's Class A or Class B license, or buy it by the bottle from one of the package sale stores owned and operated by the OLCC in nearly every community in Oregon.

In a futile attempt to legislate sob-
riety, the Oregon Legislature arbitrar-
ily limited the number of Dispenser's
Class A licenses to one for every 2000
Oregonians. They are issued to bars which
must operate in conjunction with a food
service business.

Dispenser's Class B licenses are issued
to fraternal organizations such as Elks
or Eagles Clubs. The quota does not ap-
ply to Class B licenses, and food service
is not a prerequisite.

So, if you're looking for a glass of
beer or wine in Oregon, you will find it
in a tavern, or in a pizza parlor with
the appropriate license. If you crave
a drink of something stronger, you're
looking for a bar or an Elks Club. You
can buy beer or wine to take out in nearly any grocery store or tavern, and in
many delicatessens. Hard liquor by the
bottle can be bought only in the OLCC's
green front liquor stores.

Two-thirty to seven in the morning are
dry hours in Oregon, when you can't buy
any kind of booze, anywhere.

OLCC Package Sale Stores

There are five OLCC Green Front Package Sale
Stores in Eugene and Springfield:

Eugene Agency #154
12 Willamette Plaza
343-3611

Eugene Store #45
2170 W. 6th
343-2757

Eugene Agency #169
74 Division
688-3611

Springfield Store #43
1485 Market
746-4611

Eugene Store #18
760 Charnelton
343-4424

꣰꣰꣰꣰꣰꣰꣰꣰꣰꣰꣰꣰꣰꣰꣰꣰꣰꣰꣰꣰꣰꣰꣰

On Consuming Wisely:

Most taverns sell beer by the pitcher. Where there are two sizes of pitcher available, the larger usually appears to contain twice as much beer as the smaller, giving the impression that you get more for your money when you buy the large pitcher. Appearances, however, can be deceiving, even in your neighborhood tavern.

The smaller pitcher usually contains 32 ounces of your favorite liquid, the larger either 42 ounces, 50 ounces, or 64 ounces. The trick is to know the difference, so that you don't pass up 32 ounces for $1.00, thinking that you're getting a better deal with a big (50 ounce) pitcher for $2.00.

Taylor's

894 E. 13th
342-2552

Taylor's is the closest place to the University where you can buy a beer.

Unlike most other taverns, Taylor's has a whole wall of windows. The University crowd here can watch the action on campus across the street. It is a woody, comfortable place where plants hang from the ceiling and beer drinkers sit in comfortable booths and rest their elbows on rough plank tables.

Taylor's menu is similar to that at Barney Cable's, with chili on Friday, an average hamburger and a dressed up hamburger called a Taylor-made that keeps the lunchtime crowd coming back.

The crowd is often on the scruffy side, but they're generally harmless. The music is too loud, but the service is good and the atmosphere friendly. Love affairs between professors and students often begin and end at Taylor's.

• •

Duffy's

801 E. 13th
344-3615

Duffy's is a massive fir and cedar cavern, heavily populated on weekends and evenings by hyperactive 21-year-olds who come there to lust after the same old thing while drinking beer, playing pool, and listening to music so loud it will permanently impair the hearing

143

of anyone older. Duffy's menu features soup,
sandwiches, and chili.

●●●

Max's Tavern

550 E. 13th
485-9246

Sandwiched between Wallmaster and Little's
Market, so unpretentious that you might not
notice it, is Max's, the oldest tavern in the
campus area.

This is the McSorley's of Eugene--old, smoky,
and sparse, just your basic beer-drinking establishment where Bohemians and beer drinkers
from the campus meet the Bohemians and beer
drinkers from the town. Patrons sit in small
wooden booths or along the bar on tipsy stools
rooted in the concrete floor.

Max's offers darts but no pool tables, and
you must time your trip to the john so that
you don't arrive with a dart in your shoulder.

●●●

Barney Cable's

375 E. 7th
484-7085

Free popcorn!
Barney Cable's offers free popcorn and cold
beer in a clean, comfortable, well-lighted place.

The menu here includes soup, salad, sandwiches,
and chili on Friday.

Barney Cable's is one-third pool tables, one-third pub and bar, and one-third roomy, comfortable booths where teachers, off-duty policemen, civil servants from the courthouses and the City Hall, and professional beer drinkers and workers from downtown Eugene gather for suds, company, and conversation.

•••

Luckey's Club Cigar Store

933 Olive

"The Club Cigar Store is a MAN's resort. NO LADIES REST ROOM." The dusty sign rests against the mirror behind Luckey's bar.

"That still true?" I asked the bartender, a beetle-faced old man with no hair as my wife and I sipped our beer at Luckey's bar.

"No. Wish it was." He marched grimly away from us toward the cash register. "Man can't go anywhere any more."

Luckey's, "Serving the Gentlemen of Eugene since 1911," is a relic of old Eugene, uprooted in the early 1970's from its 8th and Willamette location and transplanted uncomfortably next to the Atrium, into a neighborhood of sporting goods, ice cream, clothing, and shoe stores on Eugene's downtown mall.

"DON'T SIT ON THE TABLE!" bellowed the bartender. His voice would stop a train. Pool players froze in mid-stroke and roasted the surprised offender with glares. He slipped both feet back to the floor and play resumed.

Urban renewal financing and the Oregon Liquor Control Commission dictated the installation of

a restroom for each sex and now the unhappy bartender looks out over nearly an acre of pool
tables where men and women send little balls
ricocheting across the felt for $1.50 an hour.

There is no music at Luckey's, no soft chairs,
no low lights. People come here for the beer and
the pool.

●●●

The Harvester

1475 Franklin Boulevard
485=9274

The Harvester (formerly Murphy & Me) Tavern is
located--conveniently for thirsty joggers, bi-
cyclers, and canoers--near the mill race and the
University bike bridge, across the Willamette from
Pre's Trail. Its dark, cool, rough-sawn Douglas
fir interior is a quiet retreat for late afternoon beer drinkers.

The clientele at the Harvester is a well-bal-
anced mix of University students and professors,
workmen from nearby construction projects, truck
drivers from the Coca Cola Bottling Plant, and,
usually, a gaggle of teachers from Sheldon High
School.

The Harvester has friendly, casual help, a
soup-salad-sandwich menu, and live entertainment
most weekends. Real live roses in imported beer
bottles, pool tables, and a deck over the mill
race are other attractions that make the Harvester a nice place to visit.

●●●

Tiny Tavern

West 4th & Blair
485-9252

The Tiny Tavern is truly a neighborhood tavern,
the kind of place where you might find Archie
Bunker chewing the fat with the bartender over a
glass of beer, where everyone is on first-name
terms with everyone else. It has a genuine fireplace where beer drinkers can back up to a crackling log fire on a cold winter evening. It's an
easy-going, non-descript, comfortable place and,
though it's a Blair Avenue neighborhood institution, strangers are welcome.

••

The Cooler

20 Centennial Loop
345-6646

The Cooler is a noisy, smoke-filled quonset
hut in the parking lot behind the Coburg Road
Mayfair Grocery Store, where off-duty mechanics
and beer truck drivers gather around foosball or
pool tables or pinball machines and a couple of
old ducks copulate over the bar on a brittle
"Fly United" poster.
Posters are the main item of decoration here.
"Put the Bull Where Your Beer Is," roars a
billboard from the far wall. A "Gentleman's
Bathroom Companion" is a blond with lovely
legs squatting beside a toilet with a roll
of bathroom tissue ready on her index fingers.
"VD is nothing to clap about," we are reminded.
"Pick a winner..." is a large picture of Henry
Kissinger with a finger in his nose. A few road

signs and large color posters of comely women
in various stages of undress join large pictures
of monkeys, a few more of toilets, and one of
a naked fat lady with collossal breasts.

   Clearly, the Cooler is not a place for
feminists.

• •

The
Amber Inn
Tavern

1466 W. 7th
342-3112

   The Amber Inn is out of place, sandwiched into
a hectic limited industrial west Eugene neighborhood where all the other taverns ooze smoke and
noise and announce their presence with a blare
of pink neon. Unless you're looking for it,
you'll probably drive right by the Amber Inn.
It is a quiet, almost smokeless refuge, where
a complete menu of micro-wave meals can accompany
your beer, and couples, mostly young, relax in
small, comfortable booths.

   Before you decide never to drink in west Eugene
again, try the Amber Inn.

• •

The
Friendly Tavern

1667 W. 6th
345-6632

The Friendly Tavern is a noisy, brightly lit
place where a nearly all-male crowd of beer drinkers lurches around a couple of pool tables, shouting, shoving, swearing, and slopping beer on one
another. Others lean uncertainly from the stools
at the bar, leering at the one or two women in the
room and shouting to their pool-playing comrades.
Happiness here is in the beer. It makes a thin,
alcoholic veneer, the Saturday night face of a
frazzled, down-and-out crowd.

A small sign on the wall is an apt motto for
the Friendly Tavern: "Laugh and the world laughs
with you. Cry and you'll just dilute your beer."

• •

Side Pocket

Tavern

846 W. 6th
343-5923

The Side Pocket is a small, boxlike place
that houses an almost impenetrable wall of
smoke, three pool tables, a foosball machine,
and a dozen or so small square tables.

The smoke in here is all but immobilizing--
West 8th Street at 5:30 on Black Monday afternoon
smelled like the peak of the South Sister by
comparison--but, if your eyes and lungs can stand
it, the Side Pocket doesn't seem like a bad
place. It has the friendly feel of a neighborhood tavern, in spite of the large sign over
the bar warning "Anyone involved in a disturbance
or fighting will be prosecuted." and even offers
free pool--from 7-11 a.m.

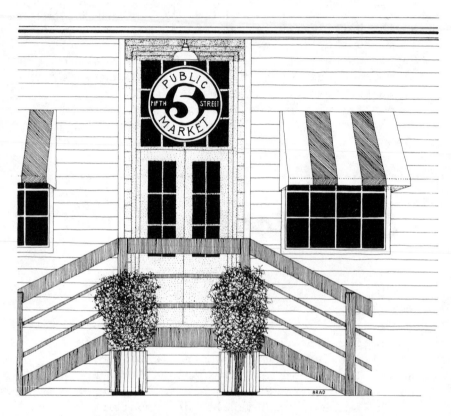

Fifth Street Public Market

Knowing Oregon's Second Market:

A Guide to Shopping in Eugene

Unique Marketplaces

* *

Saturday Market
Saturdays only
8th & Oak Streets

Hot drinks, potted plants, cold drinks, plan-
ters, wooden propellers that fly away when spun
by hand, jewelry, leather hats, cloth hats made
from old Levis, knit wool hats, knit shawls,
stuffed animals, wooden toys, stuffed cloth
trucks complete with stuffed cloth logs, welded
sculptures made by Burnt Fingers, wooden spoons,
belts, more belts, greeting cards, Cinderella
dolls--"Turn 'er upside down," bawls the salesman,
"and she's ready for the ball."--caricatures
drawn on the spot, cartoons, personal advice for
only four cents, a Mindfold, color photographs
of Oregon, belts, pots, more pots, plates and
dishes of every pottery description, more stuffed
toy animals, tie-dyed T-shirts, baggy dresses,
home-seeking puppies and kittens.
Early every Saturday morning from April to
Christmas, nearly 200 booths are nailed, bolted,
or pegged together, covered with brightly colored cloth (and plastic, if the weather threatens)
festooned with multi-colored banners, and stocked
with hand-crafted items for sale or trade on the
top deck of the county-owned parking structure
at the corner of 8th and Oak Streets, across Oak
from the Lane County Courthouse.
"Mmmmmmmmmmmmmm, boy. Piece cake. Mmmmmboy..."
The Danish pastry man promises "...five incredible

edible flavors."

"Egggggg rollllll, Eeeeeggggggg rolllll..." another vendor croons.

Falafel, calzone, pizza, root beer and do-nuts, won ton, soup and egg roll, chunichinga, lemonade, fresh fruit crepes, meatball sandwiches, knish bliss, burritoes. Food, food, food as-sails the nostrils, the belly.

Sometimes, especially on hot summer Saturday mornings, or those semi-pleasant Saturdays as Christmas approaches, the drums, the smells, the people might lure you from the mall in the center of Eugene. All Eugene rubs shoulders at the Saturday market.

Old, worn-out looking hippies--they seem to be waiting for the '60's to come back--toke bliss-fully on a Saturday morning joint while a man who might be your accountant thoughtfully con-siders the purchase of some pheasant-feather earrings and his children lose themselves in the crowd. An American Indian with a Fu Manchu beard and a Cochise haircut watches a cowboy whose beer-belly obscures his pie-plate belt buckle. Little children (Whose urchins are those?) splash through scummy puddles in the center of the market. A minstrel in ancient blue jeans and ragged beard opens a battered guitar case and his partner, a fading, spacy-looking blond with stiff, dry hair, joins him on her glittering silver flute.

A man who was almost mayor of Eugene follows his children through the throng. At the north end of the market across from the "Egggggggggrolll, eeegggggggrrrrolllllllll..." a tall black man in a flashy white suit strums a guitar and sings. Three bongo drummers and a saxophonist join him while a man in rainbow-striped pajamas leaps about almost in time to the music. Change jingles onto the pavement at the rainbow-man's feet. He picks it up and throws it into the guitarist's battered case. Three old ladies,

one with purple hair, chew egg rolls to the beat
of the bongo drums.

Saturday market smells like frying food, cigarette smoke, exhaust fumes, perfume, incense,
marijuana, cigars, sweat, and--depending on the
season--rain, snow, grass pollen and, now and then,
a patch of fresh air.

The Market is a cross-section of all Eugene's
many diverse social elements. It's a mixture of
country fair, medieval festival, and carnival with
no rides. The magic at the Saturday Market is
in the people. Don't miss it.

⌐⌐⌐⌐⌐⌐⌐⌐⌐⌐⌐⌐⌐⌐⌐⌐⌐⌐⌐⌐⌐⌐⌐⌐⌐⌐⌐

Fifth Street Public Market
296 E. 5th

The Fifth Street Public Market is a shined up,
expanded, indoor version of the Saturday Market.
It is open six days each week, Tuesday through
Sunday, all year long, at 296 E. 5th Street in
Eugene.

The original emphasis at the Fifth Street Public Market was on the marketing of handcrafted
items, but it has evolved to the point that the
craft area occupies only about one-third of the
retail space. The other space is about equally
split between eating establishments and small
shops that sell everything from books and stationery to cookware and patchwork clothing.

The Market is the best free show in town.
It's an excellent place to take a friend to
lunch, to shop for just the right handcrafted
gift for someone special, to get advice on
current books you might like to read, to buy
meat, produce, bread or wine, to have your
picture taken while you're dressed like an
old west outlaw, or just to sit and sip cof-

fee in the morning while the world parades
before your eyes. No visitor to Eugene should
leave without seeing the Fifth Street Public
Market.

What follows is a list of business establishments in the Fifth Street Public Market, divided
as the business areas are divided: eating and
crafts upstairs; groceries and et cetera downstairs.

* *

Eating at the Fifth Street Public Market

How can you not eat at the Fifth Street Public
Market? Weightwatchers must hate this place.
One step through the door and the food smells
grab you. Then you see it. All that food.
Happy people gathered round blocky little
wooden tables, eating. Eating croissants, or quiche,
or burritoes or tacoes or fat, juicy hot dogs,
shish-ke-bob, souzoukikia, spanakopeta, or maybe
a ham and cheese on rye. Thirsty? Have an
espresso or some apple juice or a milkshake.
Eat. Drink. Enjoy.

El Patio, formerly Tortilla Flat, offers
a full menu of Mexican food.

The Metropol's menu is written on butcher
paper and taped to a 6x6 post in front of the
service counter. The menu is heavily flavored
with French and features the second best French
bread in town.

Frank E. Furter sells the best hot dog in
Eugene, maybe the best in the world.

Grecian Foods features just that, Grecian foods.

The Grape Leaf Delicatessen can cater your
party or fix you a good lunch right there in
the Market.

The Epicurean Cafe not only sells good sandwiches, but it has the unique advantage of being

located in a quiet corner of the basement so you can eat your epicurean sandwich in semi-solitude.

* *

Public Market Crafts

This is no hippy belts, beads, and pots fair. Craftsmen at the Fifth Street Public Market are serious artists, working hard to produce the best of their particular craft. They are:

Beads by Vickie Buck
Bill Allord Leathercraft
Bill Simonton Candles
Bob Burt Woodcraft
Carol Krez Stained Glass
Country Studio
Empyreal Clay Trade
Eugene Leatherworks
Eugene Woolen Works
Fantasy Ventures
Fernridge Pottery
F&S Stained Glass
Gifted Hand
Heartthrob Artworks
Honeybear Leather
Ickle Deco-Tile Co.
Kay's Macrame
Light Brigade Glass Co.
Lloyd's Woodcraft
Mirific
Moonshine Copperworks
Robitai's Stained Glass
Papercuts by Ron Gentry
Portraits by Haverly
Pottery by Kathy McKeever
Pottery by Pauline Lasse
Reflections Crystal
Riverside Craft Co.
Butterfly Morning
    Women's Clothing
Carole Talbot Batiks
Oregon Rainbow Canvas Co.
Smeed's Pottery
Swans Island
Top Grain Leather Co.
Townsend Woodcraft
Under the Baobab (Batiks)
Fox Hollow Puppet Works
Scenic Oregon Originals
    (Photographs)
Wild Iris Pottery

* *

Public Market Etcetera

The following specialty shops are in the basement of the Fifth Street Public Market.

Sattva sells lampshades, lamps, and small hardwood decorative items.

One of a Kind features drawings and silkscreens by Dallas, Oregon artist R. L. Mulder.

The Patchwork Camel specializes in contemporary patchwork clothing.

The Paper Traders has a large selection of stationery, cards, games, and magazines.

Game Fair sells games.

Copper by the Pound has a large selection of copper sculptured music boxes and old copper pots and jugs from far away lands.

Fifth Street Photography will make an Old West Faded Foto featuring you all dressed up in one of their old west costumes. They also do wedding photography, restore old photographs, process and sell film, and make posters from photographs.

Folkways Imports has a large selection of woolen articles imported from Central America and Afghanistan.

The Cutting Room cuts men's and women's hair.

Our Family's a Fair sells dolls and shawls and stuffed animals.

At the Fifth Street Greenery you can get potted plants, baskets, seashells, bells, cut flowers, and dried flowers.

The Metropol Bakery sells excellent French bread, delicious eclairs, and other high quality baked goods.

Public Market Produce is the place to go for quality fruits and vegetables.

Coffee Corner is the little brother of the Coffee Corner on the upper floor. Here, in addition to coffee by the cup, you can buy all sorts of coffee paraphernalia and coffee beans and tea.

Storm Seafoods sells fish and lobster to go with a good bottle of Oregon or imported wine from its neighbor, Northwest Wine and Cheese.

You can cook up an epicurean delight in cookware from Ah...De Gaa, a cookwarehouse.

Uncommon Scents will send you away smelling

157

better than before. They sell shampoos, bubble
bath, essential perfume oils, scented glycerin
soaps, creams, lotions, and oils.

Mike O'Brien, Bibliotherapist, will advise
and sell you appropriate reading material for
yourself or for a friend at <u>Mike</u> <u>O'Brien's</u>
<u>Living</u> <u>Room</u> <u>Bookstore</u>.

¦ℙℙℙℙℙℙℙℙℙℙℙℙℙℙℙℙℙℙℙℙℙℙℙℙℙ¦

Midgley's Mill
409-445 High Street

Midgley's Mill,   one of Eugene's oldest
businesses, is now the home of seven small businesses, mostly craft-oriented, and an art gallery.

<u>Open</u> <u>Gallery</u> will probably have moved by the
time you read this. The Gallery has been occu-
pying space donated by Midgley's for the past year
or so, but Midgley is seeking a more profitable
tenant and the Open Gallery will be moving on.
Wherever it goes, it will probably continue to
be Eugene's avant garde art gallery, the scene
of new and different artistic happenings.

<u>Valley</u> <u>Potter's</u> <u>Guild</u> is the complete supply
source for anyone who makes pots.

<u>The</u> <u>Frame</u> <u>Shop</u> (see Chapter 11) frames pic-
tures or helps you to do it yourself.

<u>Midgley's</u> <u>Mill</u> sells mirrors and window-glass.

<u>Oregon</u> <u>Woodstove</u> (see chapter 11) sells wood-
stoves, stovepipe and chimney-cleaning equipment.

<u>Hamilton</u> <u>Stained</u> <u>Glass</u> is do-it-yourself
headquarters for stained glass artists.

<u>Mindy's</u> <u>Needlepoint</u> <u>Factory</u> is the headquarters
for needlepointers.

<u>Northwest</u> <u>Resource</u> <u>Recycling</u> will pick up your
cardboard or paper and pay you for it--by the ton.

Conventional
Marketplaces

* *

Valley River Center

Valley River Center is like a pedestrian Main Street, U.S.A., except that it never rains there. This climate-controlled mall has more than 100 shops, and they sell everything from books, clothes, and candles, to pipe wrenches, real estate, insurance, flowers, underwear, and cheese.

Valley River Center is a better than average place to watch people. The parade of humanity is condensed and it flows endlessly like the tide, back and forth between J. C. Penney's and Meier and Frank, Lipman's and Montgomery Ward. The best time to visit Valley River Center for people-watching is on rainy winter Saturday and Sunday afternoons; for shopping, weekday mornings after ten o'clock.

* *

Downtown Eugene

The downtown area, with the mall, a Eugene City Park, as its core, is the largest shopping center in western Oregon.

There are more than 200 stores, about 50 restaurants, play areas for children, fountains, flowers, benches for passing the time, and chess and checker boards built into little tables that rise like toadstools beneath leafy green trees. The central plaza, near the large

159

fountain, is used as a forum for a great variety
of political, social, and cultural events.
  This is the center of Eugene, at its best
on goodweather Saturday mornings when it is
crowded with people who have come to stroll and
shop and see each other.

Bargains

  The Salvage Center (3750 Franklin Boulevard)
is Eugene's best all-around second hand store.
  The Sears Surplus Store (2075 River Road, 688-
7721) sells overstocked and slightly damaged
merchandise from area Sears stores at a discount.
  The Goodwill Industries As-Is Store (3885 El-
mira Road, 689-1811) is the first stop for merchandise donated to Goodwill. At the As-Is Store
the merchandise is sold in the same condition in
which it is received. It costs less here than
the renovated merchandise sold by Goodwill in
its other two area stores. Other Goodwill Stores
are located at 72 E. 11th and 1181 Fairfield.
  France Studio (1330 Willamette, 343-2816) has
a large stock of second hand photographic equipment.
  The Buy and Sell Center (678 Olive, 344-9273)
specializes in second hand photographic and musical equipment. It also carries a fairly large
stock of second-hand miscellany.
  The Salvation Army has stores at two locations
in Eugene: 1161 Fairfield, 689-6416; and 451 W.
11th, 343-3341.
  St. Vincent De Paul has a regular store in
downtown Eugene (110 E. 11th, 344-2115) and one
in Springfield (501 Main Street, 747-5811).
St. Vincent also maintains an As-Is Store
at 1880 W. 11th, 345-0595.

The <u>Thrift</u> <u>and</u> <u>Gift</u> <u>Store</u> (2839 Willamette, 343-3861) is a second-hand store sponsored by the Junior League of Eugene. This store features slightly better quality second-hand goods. It is open during the school year from 10 to 4, Monday through Friday, and 7 to 9 on Monday evenings.

<u>H&N</u> <u>Second</u> <u>Hand</u> <u>Store</u> (86680 Franklin Boulevard, 746-7928) is a second hand store in the usual sense, but it also features antique farm and horse equipment.

If you're looking for second-hand clothes with a stylish flare or a vintage, quality look, try the following shops:

Christine's Flying Saucer
Home Furnishings--Clothier
296 Blair Boulevard

Puttin' On The Ritz
Vintage Clothing and Accessories
1639 East 19th

Rags to Riches
Second Hand Clothes
360 E. 11th

<u>Kidstuff</u> (663 Madison) is the place in Eugene for recycled children's clothing and toys.

Antiques

In Eugene, the most aggressive hunters of antiques closely watch the Miscellaneous section of the Register Guard classified ads for estate sale notices. When a <u>Worldly</u> <u>Goods</u> <u>Sales</u> <u>Service</u> or a <u>Jo</u> <u>Thayer</u> notice appears, these same people arrive at the designated address in the early morning on the first day of the sale.

The rest of us, however, ferret out bargains in Eugene's antique shops, the best of which are listed below.

Dotson's Coburg Antiques
210 N. Willamette,
Coburg 342-2732

Coburg Mercantile
155 N. Willamette,
Coburg
345-0426

Purple Lamp Antiques
89765 Green Hill Road
344-7300

Furniture Farm
5555 W. 11th
345-6841

Iron Kettle Antiques
1359 Goodpasture Island
    Road
683-1267

Marketplace Antiques
3005 Franklin Boulevard
343-3441

Copper Penny Antique Collective
2690 and 2646 Willamette
342-7986

Dianne's Antique Parlor
1850 W. 10th
345-6841

Quackenbush's
160 E. Broadway
345-8426

Turn of the Century
    Antiques
370 W. 6th
484-9661

🐲🐲🐲🐲🐲🐲🐲🐲🐲🐲🐲🐲🐲🐲🐲🐲🐲🐲🐲🐲🐲🐲🐲🐲🐲🐲🐲🐲

Fine
Wooden Furniture

The very best in contemporary woodworking craftsmanship is found in the furniture and art objects sold by the two following merchants.

Solid Ingenuity
376 E. 11th
686-1301

Made In Oregon
285 E. 5th
343-5051

🔲🔲🔲🔲🔲🔲🔲🔲🔲🔲🔲🔲🔲🔲🔲🔲🔲🔲🔲🔲🔲🔲🔲

Food

Everybody has to eat. Maybe the following information will help you to eat a little better for a little less money.

The best food prices in Eugene are found at Starflower, a feminist, worker-owned distributor of whole and organically grown foods. Starflower serves cooperatives, buying clubs, and proprietorships throughout Oregon, northern California, western Idaho, and Hawaii. You can buy from Starflower at the same price as the cooperatives. For more information on Starflower, call them at 686-2151, or write to 885 McKinley Street, Eugene 97402.

Another way to beat the supermarket price on your food is to utilize a cooperative. Membership requirements vary, but most of Eugene's cooperatives require members to put in some time working for the cooperative in order to qualify for cooperatively-priced groceries. For more information, call the following organizations:

Willamette People's Co-op
East 22nd and Emerald
343-6694

University of Oregon Food-Op
15th & Agate, on the alley
686-4911

The Grower's Market is the only totally vol-

unteer cooperative in the northwest. Food at
Grower's Market is marked up 15% over wholesale,
and the cooperative arrangement calls for one hour
of work with each order. In addition to the financial benefit, Grower's Market workers feel
that their market is a good social activity.
For more information, go to Grower's Market,
454 Willamette, or call them at 687-1145.

Produce

Though more land is eaten up each year by
housing developments, Eugene still lies in the
center of a vast agricultural area.

In the right season, produce lovers who are
smart shoppers can save a bundle by driving out
River Road or out towards Alvadore and picking
their own, or buying fresh-picked apples, beans,
blackberries, blackcaps, blueberries, cabbage,
cauliflower, cucumbers, filberts, grapes, herbs,
peaches, pears, peppers, plums, potatoes, prunes,
pumpkins, quince, raspberries, cherries, strawberries, corn, peas, tomatoes, walnuts, and probably a few more items that I can't think of
right now.

The Lane County Office of the Oregon State
University Extension Service (950 W. 13th, 687-
4243) has a wealth of information on the processing
of fresh produce. Do it right and you can enjoy
your summer harvest all winter long. While you're
at the Extension Service office, you can also
pick up a produce buyer's guide, so that you
will know where and when to look for your particular favorite.

There are plans for a farmers' market in the
Lane County Faigrounds for the summer of 1979, so,
if you can't get to the farmer, perhaps the
farmer will bring his produce to you, and you
can still skip the middleman.

Some stores have better produce year-round than the others. Among them are:

Just Produce
742 East 24th
343-5393

DJ's Markets
2750 Roosevelt Boulevard
689-2661
3305 Main, Springfield
746-4231

Public Market Produce
5th Street Public Market
296 E. 5th
342-3011

Safeway's (145 E. 18th, 350 E. 40th, and 849 West 6th) and Drive 'n' Save (2370 W. 11th and 30th & Hilyard Streets) have the best supermarket produce in Eugene.

🔲🔲🔲🔲🔲🔲🔲🔲🔲🔲🔲🔲🔲🔲🔲🔲🔲🔲🔲🔲🔲🔲🔲🔲🔲🔲

Fish

Eugene has two excellent fish markets. They are:

Storm Seafoods   Harbor Seafoods
5th Street Public Market   2417 Hilyard
296 E. 5th   686-9192
344-1927

🔲🔲🔲🔲🔲🔲🔲🔲🔲🔲🔲🔲🔲🔲🔲🔲🔲🔲🔲🔲🔲🔲🔲🔲🔲🔲

Meat

Custom Meats (577 Pearl Street, 345-4213) is
an ugly place, but the meat sold there is the
best in Eugene.

Custom Meats offers a wide variety of meats and
meat products, both with and without preservatives.
Also, if you bag a deer or an elk or a bear during
one of Oregon's big game seasons, Custom Meats
will cut, wrap, and process it to your spec-
ifications.

Specialty Foods

Porter's Foods Unlimited of Oregon (125 W.
11th) is indeed a special place. If they don't
have it in stock, they can order almost any
food product from any country in the world.
So, if you picked up a craving for a particular
brand of curry powder during your last trip to
India, Porter's can probably provide you with
it here in Eugene.

The Bamboo Pavilion (1275 Alder, 345-5788)
is a kind of oriental delicatessen, featuring
Chinese and Japanese foodstuffs, like black
mushrooms, hoisin, oyster sauce, tea, and
spices.

Cheap Bread

Four bakery thrift stores in Eugene sell old,
excess, or slightly damaged bakery products.
Pass them through your oven and they're almost

166

as good as new--at less than half the price.

Orowheat Thrift Store   Williams Bakery Thrift Stores
807 River Avenue   1760 E. 13th
                          225 River Road
Franz Thrift Store
220 Blair Boulevard

꜖ꡩꡩꡩꡩꡩꡩꡩꡩꡩꡩꡩꡩꡩꡩꡩꡩꡩꡩꡩꡩꡩꡩꡩꡩꡩꡩꡩꡩꡩꡩ

Books

Mike O'Brien's Living Room Bookstore
5th Street Public Market
296 E. 5th

    If you need a book for yourself or for a friend,
but you can't quite put your finger on a suitable
title, the place for you to go is Mike O'Brien's
Living Room Bookstore, where Mike O'Brien, Bibliotherapist, will recommend, with unusual insight,
books to suit the taste of almost any reader.
He has read most of the books in his store, and
he's had a great deal of practice reading his
customers so that he can match them with books
they will like.

The Bookmark
856 Olive
484-0512

    The Bookmark is downtown Eugene's supermar-
ket for books. Long, booklined aisles, thousands
of titles, Eugene's largest selection of new
magazines and out of town newspapers make the
Bookmark a pleasant place for browsing.

The University of Oregon Bookstore
13th & Kincaid Streets
686-4331

   The University of Oregon Bookstore is just what
you'd expect of a university bookstore. It has
the largest selection of new titles in Eugene,
paperback and hardbound, in every imaginable
subject area. It also offers a complete selection of art, writing and office supplies,
calculators, candy, T-shirts, sweat suits,
magazines, newspapers, and tennis rackets.

Book & Tea Shop
1947 E. 19th
344-3422

   The Book & Tea Shop specializes in feminist
literature, but they have abundant offerings
in nearly every other area as well, including
a very good selection of children's books. The
Book & Tea also sells tea and rolls to browsers,
and you can drink it while toasting your toes
in front of their wood fire on a cold winter
afternoon, or in the sun on their deck on a fine
spring or summer day .

The Smith Family Bookstore
768 East 13th
345-1651

   The Smith Family Bookstore is the best place
in Eugene for used books. They have over 30,000
used volumes, a good selection of new books that
they sell for 10% off the new price, new and used
magazines, and a free box where you can find books
at a price that can't be beat anywhere.

Merlin's Book Store, Limited
825 East 13th
343-4638

Merlin's Book Store, Limited, offers a profusion
of large, hardcover books, the kind with incredible
photographs that you'd like to have for yourself but they're so extravagant that you only
buy them as gifts for people you like.

Son of Koobdooga
651 East 13th
343-3551

Some people pass Son of Koobdooga daily for
years and never realize that Koobdooga is
AgoodbooK spelled backwards. Koobdooga sells
good books, hundreds of them, some magazines,
the New York Times Book Review, and children's
books and it's a pleasant place to spend enough
time to find just the right one.

J. Michael's Books
101 W. 7th
342-2002

J. Michael's Books is a used book store
where you can find a few very old, antique-
type books and a selection of regular used
paperback and hardbound books that is smaller
and generally more expensive than what you
will find at the Smith Family Bookstore.

The Kiva
136 East 11th
342-8666

Between Honey Heaven and Kiva Foods on East
11th Street is an unexpected bookstore, the Kiva.

The Kiva sells paperbacks covering a wide range
of topics and a small collection of children's
books.

Pegasus Books
1340 Alder
485-5533

   Pegasus Books, formerly The Id, has an excellent selection of travel books, and what may
be Eugene's largest selection of Cliff and Monarch
Notes. They carry an abundance of titles in
most other categoris, plus a large selection of
magazines and a few foreign-language newspapers.

Mother Kali's
541 Blair
343-4864

   "Mother Kali's is a feminist bookstore col-
lectively run by 6 wymmyn," says the shocking pink
leaflet distributed at Mother Kali's. A small
bookstore in a building that also houses a garage,
Mother Kali's carries books on childbirth, healing/
herbals, feminism, liberation movements, spiritual
reality, lesbian/gay, literature, poetry. They
have a small reading room under a stairway where
little children can leaf through "non-sexist"
children's books. They also carry posters,
cards, records, and they have a lending library on the floor above the bookstore.

Fantasy Shop
1272 Patterson
345-2568

   Superman leaps a tall building in a single bound
on the colorful sign jammed into the lawn in front

of this old house on Patterson Street. Inside
the Fantasy Shop thousands of new and used comic
books are piled on shelves that reach the high
ceilings. This is a comic book collector's heaven,
offering everything from Spiderman and Dracula
to Big Ass Comics, Zap, new and used Playboys,
and a small selection of used records.

Gandalf's Den Fantasy Gallery
99 W. 10th
484-2834

   Gandalf's Den Fantasy Gallery, a large room
on the second floor of the Atrium, specializes
in fantasy. Mind-stretching subject headings
include science fiction, heroic fantasy, light
fantasy, Middle Earth and Arthurian romance,
mystery and suspense. Gandalf's Den also sells
comic books, T-shirts, and posters.

Western Exchange
225 River Road
687-1202

   At the Western Exchange you can trade your
paperbacks or sell them. Western Exchange has
a vast selection of used paperbacks for sale
at good prices. If you're a voracious consumer
of paperback books, you're sure to find much to
like at the Western Exchange.

Walden
Valley River Center
344-9431

   Walden is the best place to shop for books
in Valley River Center. It is a good place to
browse through a vast selection of attractively

displayed titles, both paperback and hardbound.

J. K. Gill
Valley River Center
342-5518

J. K. Gill is more than 50% devoted to
stationery and office supplies, but it also
handles a fair selection of paperback fiction,
children's books, travel books, how-to books,
and a few hardbound best sellers.

The Literary Lion
84 East Broadway
687-2217

The Literary Lion is a friendly bookstore in
the Far West Federal Savings and Loan Plaza on
the mall in downtown Eugene. It is a relaxing
place with a good selection of both hardbound
and paperback titles covering nearly every
subject area.

Book Fair
1409 Oak Street
343-3303

Book Fair is by far the most cluttered used
bookstore in Eugene, in Lane County, maybe even
in Oregon. Stacks of books grow from boxes,
lean on other stacks of books which lean in turn
on cluttered bookshelves, crowd aisles and obscure windows. Paperbacks and hardbound volumes,
a few expensive rare old books, sneak into the
aisles to brush shoulders with the customers.
In the middle of all the confusion two bearded
men in blue coats, like gnomes in a forest
maze, ferret out requested volumes and ring

up sales on a noisy cash register. If your
mind is the messy attic of a booklover, you'll
love Book Fair.

Just for Kids
44 W. Broadway
484-4403

Just for Kids is the place to find the perfect
book for any child. The entire store is devoted
to making readers of little people, and it features good books for children of all ages.

🏛🏛🏛🏛🏛🏛🏛🏛🏛🏛🏛🏛🏛🏛🏛🏛🏛🏛🏛🏛

Dirty Books

Adult World
490 East Broadway
485-8923

Better hurry if you want to see this one.
Adult World is the only honest-to-goodness
dirty magazine store still in business in Eugene.
If the people who police Eugene's morality have
their way in court, it will soon be declared
a public nuisance and closed permanently.
"If nudity offends you," warns a large yellow
and black sign at the door, "please do not
enter." Inside, the walls are lined with plastic-wrapped magazines, the kind the mailman
won't leave at your house, even in a plain brown
wrapper. A display case features a few flesh-
colored, fairly lifelike "sexual aids" of
prodigious size, and there is an arcade

where--if it is ever granted a license to operate
in Eugene--you can trade your quarters for
short segments of X-rated movies.

He and She Bookstore
288 River Road
688-5711

Just outside the Eugene city limits, in the
same building that once housed the Gentleman's
Retreat, is the He and She Bookstore. The He
and She is Eugene's other dirty magazine store,
though, because it's not inside the city limits
it is not subject to the same degree of official
harassment as its cousin, Adult World. The
offering here is much the same as on the other
side of the city limits. There is a huge display
of plastic-wrapped magazines, a few books that look
like short novels, a display case of large
"marital aids" and a gloomy little theater
that shows X-rated films all day, every day,
at $4.50 per head per showing. And no popcorn.

Sleeping Around:

Where to Stay in Eugene

Sleeping Around:
Where to Stay in Eugene

   New motels don't spring up in Eugene with
the same frequency as new restaurants, but
the old ones keep getting bigger.
   The following are grouped geographic-
ally. The degree of luxury afforded by
each can be approximately gauged by the
rates charged. In addition to the
room rates, a 5% tax is levied by the
City of Eugene.

* *

Near the University of Oregon:

Black Angus Motel
2121 Franklin Blvd.
342-1243
$17-$23

Green Tree Best Western
   Motel
1769 Franklin Blvd.
484-2727
$24-$29

Maverick Motel
1859 Franklin Blvd.
342-6383
$18-$21

Rose Motel (kitchens)
969 Franklin Blvd.
345-3053
$9.95

Hyatt Lodge
1857 Franklin Blvd.
342-4804
$20-$22

Sixty Six Motel
755 E. Broadway
342-5041
$13.95-$14.95

* *

In Downtown Eugene:

Broadway Motel
659 East Broadway
344-3761
$11-$13

Mason Motel
345 W. 6th
345-3391
$15.50-$18.50

City Center Lodge Motel
476 East Broadway
344-5233
$14-$20

The Timbers Motel
1015 Pearl
343-3345
$18

Continental Motel
390 East Broadway
343-3376
$18

Travelodge
540 East Broadway
342-1109
$20-$23

Eugene Hotel*
222 East Broadway
344-1461
$19-$22

Downtown Motel
361 W. 7th
345-8739
$16-$18

Manor Motel
599 East Broadway
344-1461
$12-$16

177

In West Eugene:

Boon's Red Carpet Motel
1055 W. 6th
345-0579
$14

Texan Motel
750 W. 7th
343-3752
$11.95-$14.95

Budget Host Motor Inn
1190 W. 6th
342-7273
$12.95-$14.95

West 6th Motel
1010 West 6th
344-3747
$11-$12

El Don Motel
1140 W. 6th
344-3363
$7-$12

Notel Motel**
1190 W. 6th
343-5270
$20.95-$36.70

Executive House
1040 W. 6th
345-1343
$12.50

* *

In North-Central Eugene:

Holiday Inn
225 Coburg Road
342-5181
$27-$31

Thunderbird Motor Inn
Coburg Road & Hwy. 105
342-5201
$27-$30

* *

Near Interstate 5:

Country Squire Inn
Interstate 5, Coburg Exit
484-2000
$21-$23

Rodeway Inn
Beltline and Interstate 5
726-8181
$25-$27

Ramada Inn
Beltline and Interstate 5
726-1212
$23-$25

International Dunes
3350 Gateway
747-0332
$25

* *

Valley River Center

Valley River Inn
Valley River Center
687-0123
$34-$47

* The Eugene Hotel is Eugene's only hotel.
It is located near the center of town.

** You won't find the Notel Motel listed in
any Chamber of Commerce literature. The Notel
features water-beds, "adult" films on closed
circuit television, and day rates. And they
won't tell.

179

The Bus'll Take You There...

Getting There:

Transportation Around Eugene

ESATS and T-2000

The result of the Eugene-Springfield Area
Transportation Study (ESATS) of 1978 was the
Eugene-Springfield Area 2000 Transportation
Plan (T-2000).

When it adopted T-2000, the City of Eugene
committed itself to an attempt to pry people
away from their automobiles for at least 30%
of the trips made in the city by the year 2000.
The goal specifically translates to having 15%
of the trips made by mass transit, and another
15% made by using bicycles, by walking, or
through the use of paratransit. (There's
a new word for your vocabulary. Paratransit
refers to ride-sharing programs, such as
vanpooling, carpooling, taxis, and subscription bus service.)

Springfield, in a move that is characteristic
of that city, adopted the more modest goal of
10% mass transit ridership. The Springfield
City Council then revised the goal downward
to 5%. They have no specific goal for transportation modes other than mass transit.

* *

The Automobile

Eugene covers 28 square miles. As in other
cities, much land has been devoted to making the
city accessible by automobile. Total street
mileage inside the city is 316.62 miles, 297.5
of which are paved or surfaced. Free parking is
a feature of most shopping areas in the city,
including Valley River Center and downtown
Eugene which has, in addition to abundant street-
side parking, two multi-storied concrete parking

182

facilities which offer free parking.

Eugene is located on Interstate 5, the main north-south route for traffic in the western states. The city is 114 miles south of Portland and 216 miles north of the California border. Westbound traffic from Eugene flows through the Coast Range sixty miles on Highway 126 to the Pacific Coast at Florence where it joins Highway 101. Eastbound traffic from Eugene climbs through the Cascade Range on either Highway 58, through the Willamette Pass, or Highway 126, through the Santiam Pass. Highway 126, the northernmost of the two routes, links with Highway 20 near the Santiam Pass and is the most direct route to Bend, Oregon. Highway 58 joins Highway 97 about 20 miles beyond the Willamette Pass and is the most direct route to Klamath Falls.

From Eugene easy day trips by automobile are possible to the Pacific Coast, to recreational areas in the Cascade Mountains, and to Portland, Oregon's largest city. (See Chapter 4 for more on day trips from Eugene.)

* *

The Bus'll Take You There.

Lane Transit District buses will take you almost anywhere in the Eugene-Springfield area, economically and comfortably. Everybody knows that. But, say you want to go fishing up the McKenzie River and you don't have a car. The

bus'll take you there, as far as Blue River,
for $1.10 each way. You can take the early morn-
ing bus up the river, fish all day, and catch
the evening bus back into Eugene. Want to visit
your cousin in Marcola or your girl friend in
Junction City? The bus'll take you there, too.

Out of town fares vary, but around the town
it costs 35¢ each way for anyone over 11 years
old, 15¢ for children between 5 and 11. If you're
under five years old you ride free.   The drivers
don't make change, so you should have exact
change or a token ready when you board the
bus.

LTD also has a Dial-A-Bus service for
people confined to wheelchairs or whose mobility
is limited in other ways. If you want to take
advantage of the Dial-A-Bus you must make re-
servations 24 hours in advance of the time you
wish to ride.

For information on regular LTD schedules and
fares, call 687-5555. To call the Dial-A-Bus,
dial 687-5566.

* *

Bike it.

In 1975 Lane County and the cities of Eugene
and Springfield adopted the Metropolitan Bikeway
Master Plan. This plan calls for the completion
of about 175 miles of bikeways throughout the
metropolitan area by 1990, the bulk of which
will be within the Eugene city limits.

Eugene has committed itself to constructing
150 miles of bikeways, over 50 miles of which
are now completed. Bicyclists can travel safely
and swiftly to most destinations in Eugene,
using designated bikeways.

The Eugene Public Works Department (City
Hall II, 858 Pearl Street) distributes an excellent

184

free map of Eugene Area Bikeways. They also have some people who will answer your questions about the bikeway program. Call them at 687-5928.

Bicyclists riding on public thoroughfares in Oregon are subject to the same laws as are drivers of other vehicles, and they have the same rights. Remember, though, that when a bicyclist on his 25 pound vehicle collides with a 3000 pound Chrysler, the question of who had the right-of-way is fairly unimportant. There are no old beligerent bicycle riders.

To be safe:

(1) Be visible. This means being sure that your bicycle has the appropriate lights and reflectors and that you are dressed in light-colored clothing when riding at night.

(2) Be predictable. Always signal well in advance of turning. Make sure the driver of the car behind you or coming at you knows what you are going to do before you do it. It's not smart to fool cars.

(3) Obey all the traffic laws. This means doing those pesky little things like travelling on the right side of the road and stopping at stop signs.

(4) Be smart. A little common sense may save your life.

* *

Foot it.

A pedestrian is in touch with his or her environment in a way that drivers of automobiles never are.

While drivers, in their iron cages, are contending with each other's foul moods, backed up 50 cars from the Ferry Street Bridge at 5:00 on a Friday afternoon, a walker can admire a lovely old house, or sense the passage of the seasons by noticing the first green leaf in the spring, the smell of a rosebush near the sidewalk, or the first tinge of red-orange in the shrubbery that portends the coming of fall.

A walker can watch a majestic heron, fishing stilt-legged in the Willamette, surprise a raccoon or possum swaggering through an alley in search of left-over cat food, or watch a beaver determinedly gnaw through a tree in Alton Baker Park. A walker can even, in this impersonal time, speak to his neighbor. He can smell an approaching storm, hear little children on an elementary school playground, or wander at his own pace through the mad rush of commerce on the downtown sidewalks. In short, a walker in Eugene can lead an interesting life.

The Eugene Pedestrian Report, published by the City of Eugene in December, 1977, in conjunction with the development of T-2000, says that Eugene has decided to place greater emphasis on the walking mode in future transportation systems. The report points out that there are 159 miles of streets with inadequate sidewalks in Eugene, and recommends that sidewalks be installed and improved, especially within walking distance of the schools, in order to encourage more people, especially students who are now bused, to walk.

There are, then, 157.62 miles of perfectly adequate sidewalks in Eugene. In addition, the pedestrian in Eugene can choose from a variety of interesting alleyways, bike paths, malls, footpaths, and even saw-dust jogging trails, and incorporate them all into a personally viable transportation system.

With all this, why idle away so much of your life isolated, like a canned vegetable, from such an interesting and stimulating environment?

Get out of that car. Walk.

* *

Call Me a Taxi.

   Taxi rates in Eugene are set by the Eugene
City Council. Though they, like everything else,
continue to spiral upward, at this writing a
taxi ride in Eugene will cost you 80¢ per mile,
plus a dollar "flag drop" charge when you get
into the taxi. There are four taxi companies in
Eugene:

Dial Cab Company
1125 Bailey Hill Road
342-5222

Eugene Airport Limousine Service
746-1440

Eugene Taxi Service
343-7711

Ricksha Taxi
1160 W. 8th
484-9831

* *

In the month of november last we
had a full of some 2 inches of snow one
night--the next morning it looked
Irregular to see Tomato Pumpkin Cucumbers & Bean blossoms Peering through
the Snow it was all gone by ten o'clock
and the vine Continued to blossom until
about the middle of Dec....Ice formed on
the ponds...none in the stream, to
the thickness of 3 inches which the
boys used for skating....my Peach &
Almond trees are in full bloom StrawburyBloom have been seen every month
this winter....

Stock require little or no feed
in Oregon in winter unless near a town.
I have some 100 h of cows & stock
cattle and they have no feed this
winter except what nature provides...

Eugene Skinner
to his sister
March 18, 1860

It Doesn't Rain All the Time:

Eugene's Weather

It Doesn't Rain <u>All</u> The Time:
A Guide to Eugene's Weather

The following information is taken, word for word, from the <u>Local Climatological Data Annual Summary With Comparative Data</u> for 1977. It is the most current climatological information available at the time of this writing. The <u>Summary</u> is published by the National Oceanic and Atmospheric Administration's Environmental Data Service from information compiled at the office of the National Weather Service at Mahlon Sweet Field, nine miles northwest of Eugene.
   The report:

Eugene is located at the upper or southern end of the fertile Willamette Valley. Mahlon Sweet Field, location of the National Weather Service Office, is nine miles northwest of the city center.
   The Cascade Mountains to the east and the Coast Range to the west bound the valley, and low hills to the south nearly close it, but northward the level valley floor broadens rapidly. Hills of the rolling, wooded Coast Range begin about five miles west of the air-port and rise to elevations of 1500 to 2500 feet midway between Eugene and the Pacific Ocean lying 50 miles to the west. About ten miles east, the Coburg Hills, rising to an elevation of 2500 feet, obscure snow-covered peaks of the Cascade Range, which reach elevations of 10,000 feet about 75 miles away. Small valleys extend into the hills in all directions and hard-surfaced highways, through passes in the Cas-cades, provide easy access to winter sports areas.
   Abundant moisture and moderate temperatures result in rapid growth of evergreen timber and lumbering is a major industry. Much of the virgin timber has been harvested, but new growth

190

springs up quickly so there is very little bare ground and duststorms are unknown.

The Willamette River passes about five miles east of the airport and Fern Ridge flood control reservoir, with a normal pool of 9360 acres, begins about two miles southwest. These two water areas are the main source of local fog, but numerous small creeks and low places, which fill with water in the wet season, also produce considerable fog. The Coast Range acts as a barrier to coastal fog, but active storms cross these ridges with little hindrance. The Cascade Range blocks westward passage of all but the strongest continental air masses, but when air does flow into the valley from the east, dry, hot weather develops in summer causing extreme fire hazard. In winter this situation causes clear, sunny days and cool frosty nights.

Wind

The centers of low barometric pressure, with which rain is associated, generally pass inland north of Eugene and as a result southwest winds with speeds of ten to twenty mph usually accompany rainfall. Heavier storms bring winds of thirty to forty mph and occasional southwest winds exceeding fifty mph are experienced. Fair weather in both summer and winter is most often accompanied by calm nights and daytime northerly winds increasing to speeds of five to fifteen mph in the afternoon.

Mean Wind Speed (mph)

Jan.	Feb.	Mar.	Apr.	May	Jun.	
8.3	7.9	8.6	7.7	7.4	7.4	

Jul.	Aug.	Sep.	Oct.	Nov.	Dec.	Year
8.0	7.5	7.4	6.6	7.1	7.7	7.6

Rain and Snow

The change in seasonal rainfall is quite gradual. The first fall rains usually arrive in the second or third week of September, after which rain gradually increases until about the first of January and then slowly decreases to the latter part of June. July and August are normally very dry, occasionally passing without rainfall.

When snow occurs, it frequently melts on contact with the ground or within a few hours, but occasionally an accumulation of a few inches will persist as a ground covering for several days. Snowfall for a winter season exceeds five inches in about one-third of the years. There have been a few instances of an entire winter without so much as a trace of snow, while at the other extreme, snowfall exceeded three feet for the 1915-1916, 1949-1950, and the 1968-1969 seasons. In January 1950 snow on the ground reached a depth of eight inches and maintained a cover for 11 days. Nineteen years later 47.1 inches of snow in January, 1969, accumulated to a depth of 34 inches on the ground with a cover of an inch or more persisting for 19 days.

Record Mean Precipitation

Jan.	Feb.	Mar.	Apr.	May	Jun.	
7.95	5.05	5.19	2.44	1.93	1.26	

Jul.	Aug.	Sep.	Oct.	Nov.	Dec.	Year
0.30	0.76	1.35	3.83	6.76	7.71	44.53

Record Mean Snowfall

Jan.	Feb.	Mar.	Apr.	May	Jun.	(T=trace)
5.0	0.4	0.7	T	T	0.0	

Jul.	Aug.	Sep.	Oct.	Nov.	Dec.	Year
0.0	0.0	T	T	0.3	1.2	7.6

Temperature

Temperatures are so largely controlled by maritime air from the Pacific that long periods of extremely hot or severely cold weather never occur. Maximums of 95 degrees or higher have occured only in the months of June, July, August, and September, averaging three days a year. Minimums of twenty degrees or lower are infrequent, averaging five per year. The temperature has lowered to 32 degrees or below as late as June 13 and as early as September 24, but the average dates of their last occurrence in the spring and first occurrence in the fall are April 9 and October 31.

Average Temperature (farenheit)

	Jan.	Feb.	Mar.	Apr.	May	Jun.
Mean	39.5	43.3	45.6	49.8	55.6	61.2
Max.	45.9	51.4	54.7	60.7	67.7	74.1
Min.	33.0	35.2	36.5	38.9	43.4	48.2

	Jul.	Aug.	Sep.	Oct.	Nov.	Dec.	Annual
Mean	66.8	66.2	62.0	53.0	45.6	41.2	52.5
Max.	82.5	81.4	76.6	64.0	53.0	47.2	63.3
Min.	51.0	51.0	47.4	42.0	38.1	35.2	41.7

Agriculture and Climate

The long growing season and mild temperatures
are favorable for diversified agriculture and
numerous crops are commercially important. Due
to high ground water level, pumping of irrigation
water is economical and sprinkling of cannery
crops and berries is the general practice;
also numerous pastures are irrigated. Table
beets, green beans, sweet corn, carrots, and
pumpkins are processed in large quantities.
Peaches, pears, cherries, plums, berries, and
rhubarb are also canned, with cherries and pears
comprising the greater pack. Other agricultural
products are apples, prunes, peppermint, spearmint,
tomatoes, and cucumbers. Nonirrigated ranches
and farms produce large amounts of hay, grain,
grass seed, livestock, tree fruits, and nuts.

Living Better:

A Few Things Every Eugenean Should Know

Living Better:
A Few Things
Every Eugenean Should Know

   Included among the jumble of odds
and ends that follow are some opinions
and information that I've acquired
during nearly ten years in Eugene.
Much of this information was picked
up after extended periods of trial
and error. When I finally came to
the conclusions that follow, I often
wondered, "Why didn't somebody just
tell me that, before I...?"

● ●

   After a Humble Bagel (Humble Bagel Company,
2435 Hilyard, 484-1142) all others taste like
day old bread.

   Pipes plugged? When your little boy flushes
his diaper away, you'll need someone to turn to.
La-Z-Drains (Mack Sims, owner, 484-1949) will
retrieve the diaper and free up your sewer system
quickly for about half what most of his competition
will charge.

   Need a realtor? Try Hugh Prichard (Mountain
Valley Real Estate, 1175 Charnelton, 484-5166)
or Bob McCulloch (J. J. Meier Company, 29 W.
29th, 484-0001) They are honest, reliable, and
knowledgeable men who will help you solve your
real estate problems whether you're buying or
selling.

   The best hot dog in Eugene is at Frank E.
Furter's (5th Street Public Market, 296 East
5th). A dollar and a quarter buys a fat, juicy

frank and all the relish, onions, mustard, and
ketchup you'll ever need in a bun that doesn't
fall apart when you pick it up.

The Frame Shop (in Midgley's Mill, 417 High
Street, 687-1949) is the place to go when you
want a picture framed. They'll either do it
for you or, for $1.00 per picture, they'll let
you use their tables and tools and tell you
how to do it right.

Though they'll probably deny it, it is cheaper
to mail packages at the University Branch of the
U. S. Postal Service (in the Erb Memorial Union
on the southeast corner of 13th and University
Streets, 687-6636). A package mailed at the
Main Branch downtown for 42¢ goes at the University
Branch for 28¢. Also, the University Branch is
usually deserted early on Saturday mornings and
you'll be able to do your postal business quickly
here at that time.

Starflower (885 McKinley, 686-2151), the women's
collective mentioned in the shopping section of
this book, has the best food prices in town.
You have to buy in bulk, but the savings make it
worth the extra effort.

Prince Puckler's (two locations--in the Atrium
at 99 West 10th, 343-2621, or at 1473 E. 19th,
343-8023) has the best ice cream anywhere.

Need a plumber for your new house or for an
addition to an old one? Mike Stimac (344-2407)
is a plumbing contractor who will do it better.

Never had hay fever? Maybe you've just never
been in Eugene in the springtime. Our rainforest
bursts into bloom in May and June, filling
the air with pollen. Noses run, eyes itch,
thousands of Eugene residents spend their nights

197

coughing, sneezing, and rubbing their eyes instead
of sleeping. The worst days are those lovely hot
early summer days when the wind blows in from
the grass fields north of the city, adding
rye grass pollen to the dust, exhaust fumes and
pollen already in the city air. Eugene has one
of the highest pollen counts in the world on such
days. Want relief? Get out of town. Go to the
coast, the mountains, anywhere out of the valley
and you'll feel better.

The 4th of July is more important to hay fever
sufferers in Eugene than it is to most people.
Usually, right after the 4th, the air is breath-
able again and hay fever sufferers put away their
handkerchiefs until the following spring.

The James G. Blaine Society is named for a man
who never set foot in Oregon. Members of the
Society hope they can persuade others to follow
his example.

Schools in Eugene District #4J offer a wide
diversity of programs to residents of the school
district. District #4J has an open enrollment
policy. This means that a student need not live
in the attendance area of the school he or she
attends. Any student may attend any school in
the district on a space-available basis. Some
mothers of small children spend each spring
shopping through the elementary schools for just
the right teacher for their child for the
following year. High school students who are
serious about drama might transfer to Sheldon
High School because of the reputation of
Sheldon's drama program.

District #4J offers its students a smorgas-
bord of educational opportunity. The student
who takes advantage of the open enrollment policy assumes the responsibility for transportation
to the chosen school.

For more information, call 687-3327.

The best deal in home heating in Eugene is
firewood.   The U. S. Forest Service (687-6251)
or the Bureau of Land Management (687-6651)
can tell you where to go to gather you own for
free or for 50¢ a cord.   A cord of wood is a
stack 4'x4'x8'.   As Thoreau discovered, wood
warms you twice--once when you cut it and again
when you burn it.   That's a great deal of heat
for 50¢.

A crackling fire in a fireplace is an aesthetic
pleasure but, in the long run, will do little to
lessen your dependence for heat on the oil companies or the Eugene Water and Electric Board.
For maximum wood heating efficiency, you need
a woodstove.

For a hard-working, heavy duty, made-in-
America woodstove, you can't beat a Fisher Stove
(Fisher Stoves International, Inc., 1500 Valley
River Drive, 686-8424;   Fisher Stoves and Antiques,
4213 Main Street in Springfield, 747-3841).
Next to a Fisher, most of the other American-made
woodstoves seem like leaky pieces of tin.   For
the more delicate European models, try the Oregon Woodstove Company (411 High Street, 484-6474).

Hit a rock with your chain saw?   The man at
Mercury Equipment (2060 W. 7th Place, 484-0514)
knows everything there is to know about chain
saws and he can fix your old one or sell you
a new one.

When you get around to building your dream
home, call Gary Folker or Elmer Vaughan (Drift
Creek Construction, 688-5273, or, a Creswell
number, 1-895-2567).   Custom houses already built
by Drift Creek can be seen at 1609, 1611, and
1617 East 43rd, and a little farther up 43rd
on the other side of the road.   They'll work
with you on your plans and financing and you'll

get quality, custom construction at a reasonable price.

If your American-made car needs a good mechanic, try Joe's Garage (888 W. 1st, 343-1814). That they are honest and competent isn't exactly a secret in Eugene, so you'll have to call well in advance for an appointment.

You can buy nearly anything for just a little bit less at BiMart (1680 W. 18th, 342-2687; 1521 Mohawk Boulevard in Springfield, 746-9637; 2030 River Road, 689-3551). Membership costs $2.00 but you'll probably save that much on your first shopping trip.

If your chimney doesn't draw properly, it may be dangerously dirty. For a chimney-cleaning with a theatrical touch, try David Stuart Bull (The Jolly Good Chimney Sweep, 897 Fox Glenn, 344-5571).

Anyone interested in wildlife in Oregon will benefit from a free subscription to Oregon Wildlife, a magazine published monthly by the Oregon State Department of Fish and Wildlife. To subscribe, write to the Oregon Department of Fish and Wildlife, PO Box 3503, Portland, Oregon 97208.

Nudity, or, more specifically, the exposure by anyone eight years old or older of his or her genitals to another person, is prohibited on public or private property in Lane County, "except within the boundaries of private property with the permission of the owner of said property, that is screened so that it cannot be viewed from any other property". The nudity ordinance was added to the Lane County Code in 1976, in response to complaints by land-owners and picnickers that large numbers of people were skinny-

dipping in the McKenzie and Willamette Rivers and
their tributary streams. Though questions abound
about the specific interpretation of the ordinance,
one interpretation is that it prohibits nudity
even in a public shower, and another is that it
unfairly discriminates against men because their
genitals are more readily visible than women's.

Violation of the ordinance is punishable by
a maximum fine of $1000 and thirty days in jail.
In Springfield, not only is it "...unlawful
for any person to intentionally expose or exhibit
his or her sexual organs..." but it is also un-
lawful "...in the case of a female person, to
wholly expose her breasts in any public place
or private place open to public view from either
public or adjacent private property". The Springfield code adds, ominously, "The conduct herein
regulated need be witnessed by only one person."
In the "You Ain't Seen Nothin' Yet" Department, the Florence City Council has made it un-
lawful to have sexual intercourse within the
city limits. A Florence man whose wife was
due to give birth to their baby recently requested a variance from the ordinance. The City
Council granted the variance.
And, though it did not happen in Eugene or
Lane County, the following story did happen in
Oregon and is perhaps the best way to end this
little section. The Stanfield, Oregon, City
Council, in 1975, enacted a law making it il-
legal for animals to engage in sex acts in public
view. Owners of animals who violate the pro-
visions of this ordinance are liable to be fined
$15 of sentenced to from two to 25 days in the
city jail.

WHITE BIRD

White Bird Clinic

Resources:
Someone
To Turn To

Your Elected Representatives

* *

National

President of the United States
> Jimmy Carter (Democrat)

United States Senators
> Mark Hatfield (Republican)
> Robert Packwood (Republican)

United States Representative, Fourth Congressional District
> James Weaver (Democrat)

* *

State

Governor
> Vic Atiyeh (Republican)

Secreatary of State
> Norma Paulus (Republican)

State Treasurer
> Clay Myers (Republican)

Attorney General
> James A. Redden (Democrat)

Superintendent of Public Instruction
> Verne Duncan

Labor Commissioner
> Mary Roberts (Democrat)

State Senators
> George Wingard (Republican)
> > District 20
> Edward Fadely (Democrat)
> > District 21
> Ted Kulongoski (Democrat)
> > District 22

State Representatives
                    Grattan Kerans (Democrat)
                        District 39
                    David Frohnmayer (Republican)
                        District 40
                    Mary Burrows (Republican)
                        District 41
                    Nancie Fadeley (Democrat)
                        District 42
                    Larry Campbell (Republican)
                        District 43
                    Bill Rogers (Republican)
                        District 44

    The Oregon State legislature convenes on the
second Monday in January in odd-numbered years.
State officials are elected in even numbered years
and sworn in the following January.
* *

County

Lane County Commissioners
    Vance Freeman (Springfield)
    Gerald Rust (South Eugene)
    Harold Rutherford (West Lane)
    Otto t'Hooft (East Lane)
    Archie Weinstein (North Eugene)

    Lane County Commissioners meet Wednesdays at
9 a.m. in Harris Hall at the Lane County Courthouse.

District Attorney
    Pat Horton
Lane County Sheriff
    David Burks
Lane County Assessor
    William Bain

* *

City

Mayor
  Gus Keller
City Council
  Ward 1-Emily Schue
  Ward 2-Betty Smith
  Ward 3- Jack Delay
  Ward 4-Gretchen Miller
  Ward 5- D. W. Hamel
  Ward 6-Eric Haws
  Ward 7-Scott Lieuallen
  Ward 8- Brian Obie

The Eugene City Council meets the second and fourth Mondays of each month at 7:30 p.m. in the City Council Chamber at the Eugene City Hall, and every Wednesday at noon at the Oakway Mall King's Table Restaurant.

Eugene Water and Electric Board Commissioners
  At Large-Jack Craig
  Wards 1&8-John Tiffany
  Wards 2&3-Camilla Pratt
  Wards 4&5-John Bartels
  Wards 6&7-Richard Freeman

The Eugene Water and Electric Board Commissioners meet on the first Monday of each month at 7:30 p.m. and the third Monday of each month at 12:30 p.m. at 500 E. 4th Street.

* *

Lane County Board of Education (Educational Service District)
  At Large-Jack Billings
          Nile Williams
Zone 1 (School District #4J)
  Cynthia Wooten

206

Zone 2 (School Districts 19, 68, 79)
    Jeanne Armstrong
Zone 3 (School Districts 1, 40, 45J, 71, 76)
    Hugh Peniston
Zone 4 (School Districts 28J, 32, 66, 90, 97J)
    Beverly Ficek
Zone 5 (School Districts 52, 69)
    Cleve Dumdi

The Lane County Board of Education meets
the second and fourth Tuesdays of each month
at the Administrative Offices, 1200 Highway 99N,
Eugene.

∞∞∞∞∞∞∞∞∞∞∞∞∞∞∞∞∞∞∞∞∞

Lane Community College Board of Education
At Large   Larry Perry
                Leslie Hendricksen
Zone 1   Edward E. Cooper
Zone 2   James Pitney
Zone 3   Charlene Curry
Zone 4   Stephen Reid
Zone 5   Catherine Lauris

The Lane Community College Board of Education
meets the second Wednesday of each month in the
Board Room at Lane Community College, 4000 E.
30th Avenue, at 7:30 p.m.

Eugene School District #4J Board of Education
    James Britton (Chairman)
    James Jeppeson (Vice Chairman)

Margaret Gontrum
Donna Kernutt
~~Frank Nearing~~
Howard Warner
~~Jonathon West~~

The Board of Education of Eugene School District
#4J meets the first and third Mondays of each
month at 7:30 p.m. at the Education Center, 200
North Monroe, Eugene.

Bethel School District #52 Board of Education
    Glenna McWhorter (Chairman)
    Jerry Carter (Vice Chairman)
    Lee Brown
    Milton Decker
    Irene DePaepe
    John Hulsey
    Pat Munkres

The Board of Education of Bethel School District
#52 meets the second and fourth Mondays of each
month at 7:30 p.m. at the Administration Building,
4640 Barger Avenue, Eugene.

* *

Communicate with your elected officials

To communicate with your elected officials,
write them at the appropriate address listed
below.

The White House
Washington, D. C. 20500

United States Senate
Washington, D. C. 20510

House of Representatives
Washington, D. C. 20515

Capitol Building
Salem, Oregon 97310

Lane County Courthouse
125 E. 8th
Eugene, Oregon 97401

Eugene City Hall
777 Pearl
Eugene, Oregon 97401

Eugene Water and Electric Board
500 E. 4th Street
Eugene, Oregon 97401

Eugene School District #4J
200 N. Monroe
Eugene, Oregon 97401

Bethel School District #52
4640 Barger Avenue
Eugene, Oregon 97402

Lane Educational Service District
1200 Highway 99N
Eugene, Oregon 97402

Lane Community College
400 E. 30th
Eugene, Oregon 97405

* *

Political Party Headquarters in Eugene

Democratic Party Headquarters
708 Washington
Eugene, Oregon 97401
Telephone 687-1573

Libertarian Party Headquarters
385 E. 11th
Eugene, Oregon 97401
Telephone 484-1202

Republican Party Headquarters
96 E. Broadway
Eugene, Oregon 97401
Telephone 484-1872

* *

Meeting Days

Lane Council of Governments   687-4283
   Meets the fourth Thursday of each month at
   7:30 p.m. No fixed location, but the location is announced in the press prior to
   each meeting.

Lane County Local Government Boundary Commission
                                           686-7860
   Meets the first Thursday of each month at 7:30
   p.m. in the Eugene City Hall Council Chamber.

Lane County Mass Transit District   687-5581
    Meets the third Tuesday of each month at 7:30
    p.m. at the Eugene City Hall.

Lane County Planning Commission   687-4186
    Meets the second and fourth Tuesdays of each
    month at 7:00 p.m. in Harris Hall, Lane County
    Courthouse.

Lane Regional Air Pollution Authority 686-7618
    Meets the second Tuesday of each month at
    noon in the Authority Conference Room, 16
    Oakway Mall, Eugene.

Eugene Downtown Development Board   687-5443
    Usually meets on the first Wednesday of the
month at 7:30 a.m., in the McNutt Room, Eugene

Eugene Downtown Development Board   687-5443
    Usually meets on the first Wednesday of the
    month at 7:30 a.m., in the McNutt Room, Eugene
    City Hall.

Eugene Community Development Committee 687-5443
    Meets on the second Thursday of each month at
    11:30 a.m. at the Thunderbird on Coburg Road,
    Eugene.

Eugene Joint Housing Committee   687-5443
    Meets monthly. Time and location are announced
    in the newspaper.

Urban Renewal Agency of the City of Eugene
                                687-5443
    Meets the first and third Thursdays of each
    month at 10 a.m., usually in the McNutt Room,
    Eugene City Hall.

Eugene Human Rights Council   687-5010
    Meets the last Thursday of each month at 7:30
    p.m., in the McNutt Room, Eugene City Hall.
    Individual commissions also meet monthly.
    For information on the following Commissions,
    call 687-5010.
            Commission on the Rights of the Aging
            Commission on the Rights of the Handicapped
            Commission on the Rights of Minorities
            Commission on the Rights of Women
            Youth Commission

* *

Neighborhood Organizations

If you are concerned about the effects of growth
and change on your neighborhood, perhaps you should
work with your neighborhood group to maximize your
clout when it comes time to form policies affect-
ing your neighborhood at Eugene City Hall.

Active Bethel Citizens
660 Hughes
Eugene 97402
689-3009, 688-5098

Amazon Neighbors
2760 University
Eugene 97403
345-2205, 687-4271

Cal Young Neighborhood
    Association
1312 Piper Lane
Eugene 97401
484-4904, 689-0911

Fairmount Neighbors
2595 Highland Drive
Eugene 97403
343-7311

Far West Neighborhood
    Association
1215 Arthur
Eugene 97402
686-3610

Friendly Area Neighbors
840 W. 22nd
Eugene, 97405
687-0094, 345-6787

Churchill Neighborhood
   Association
2474 Blackburn
Eugene, 97405
484-9053

Crest Drive Citizens
   Association
794 Crest Drive
Eugene 97405
343-1357, 485-8353

Dunn Neighbors
3101 Willamette
 Eugene 97405
343-0357

East Skinner Butte
   Friends and Neighbors
235 E. 3rd
Eugene 97401

Oak Hills Homeowners
   Association
2002 Kimberley
Eugene 97405
342-3863, 686-8030

South Hills Neighborhood
   Association
430 E. 46th
Eugene 97405
344-3430

South University Neigh-
   borhood Association
1845½ University
Eugene 97403
345-3757

Harlow Neighbors
953 Van Duyn
Eugene 97401
343-5561, 687-8388

Hawkins Highland
   Neighborhood
   Organization
2090 Broadview
Eugene 97405
344-0959

Jefferson Area Neighbors
2887 Potter
Eugene 97405
345-1493

Laurel Hill Valley
   Citizens Committee
1840 Augusta
Eugene 97403
345-2228

West University Neigh-
   bors
1280 Mill
Eugene 97401
345-1159

Westside Neighbor-
   hood Quality Project
591 W. 10th
Eugene 97401
345-3277

Whiteaker Community
   Council
1190 W. 5th
Eugene 97402
345-2663

Southeast Firs Neighbor-
hood Association
4970 Whiteaker
Eugene 97405
484-2262, 484-7007

* *

Groups Chartered by Lane County

Just as the neighborhood organizations were formed to affect policy-making in Eugene, the following organizations and groups were formed to affect policy-making by the Lane County Commissioners.

Fir Butte-Oak Hill Community Organization
88648 Fir View
Eugene 97402
689-0508

Greater Fox Hollow Valley Association
29236 Fox Hollow Road
Eugene 97405
344-0949

River Road Community Organization
115 Elkay Drive
Eugene 97404
689-6208

Santa Clara Community Organization
83 Kingsbury
Eugene 97402
688-4050, 484-8422

Seavey Loop United Group
86136 Garden Valley
Eugene 97405
746-3430

Spencer Butte Improvement Association
31458 Fox Hollow Road
Eugene 97405
345-3962

Spencer Creek Planning and Zoning Committee
29141 Spencer Creek Road
Eugene 97405
343-4483

* *

Community Schools

Eugene's community schools are central places around which neighborhoods revolve. Each community school has a program that is unique to that building and is designed to serve its neighborhood. These programs may take the form of classes in yoga or pottery or nutrition, or they may be as simple as making a gymnasium availble for a women's volleyball team practice or a YBA basketball game. They are places in each neighborhood where neighbors get together to learn and have fun.

Coburg Community School
Brownsville Road
Coburg 97401
687-3412

Dunn Community School
3411 Willamette

Eugene 97405
687-3482

Edison/Eastside Community School
1328 East 22nd
Eugene 97403
687-3284

Laurel Hill Community School
2621 Augusta
Eugene 97403
687-3288

Lincoln Community School
650 W. 12th
Eugene 97402
687-3485

Madison Community School
875 Wilkes Street
Eugene 97404
687-3278

Patterson Community School
1510 Taylor
Eugene 97402
687-3542

Whiteaker Community School
21 N. Grand
Eugene 97402
687-3505

Willagillespie Community School
1125 Willagillespie Road
Eugene 97401
687-3362

Willard Community School
2855 Lincoln
Eugene 97405
687-3509

Community Resource and Involvement Program
Churchill High School
1850 Bailey Hill Road
Eugene 97405

* *

Ethnic Groups

The following groups provide aid, education, or advocacy for members of their particular ethnic group.

Asian American Student Union
EMU
University of Oregon
Eugene 97403

Black Student Union
Suite 14, EMU
University of Oregon
Eugene 97403

Chicano Affairs Center
1326 Lawrence, #6
Eugene 97401

Eugene Indian Center
795 Willamette, Room 222
Eugene 97401

Eugene Native American Solidarity
541 Blair
Eugene 97402

Indian Education Project
School District 4J
200 N. Monroe
Eugene 97402

Indian Program on Alcohol and Drug Awareness
1632 Columbia
Eugene 97403

MECHA
Moviemento Estudiantil Chicanos de Aztlan
EMU
University of Oregon
Eugene 97403

Native American Student Union
EMU Suite 14B
University of Oregon
Eugene 97403

* *

Technological Alternatives

The following groups are seeking to improve our environment by encouraging ecologically sound alternatives to traditional practices which are harmful to the environment. They are concerned with recycling, with lobbying for legislation with favorable impact upon the environment, and with the utilization of agricultural methods which are practical and profitable but not harmful to man or to the soil.

Amity Foundation
2760 Riverview
Eugene 97403
484-7171

Aprovecho Institute
359 Polk
Eugene 97402
345-5981

Eugene Future Power Committee
PO Box 5274
Eugene 97405

Solar Energy Center
1545 Agate
Eugene 97403

Oregon Appropriate Technology
PO Box 5388
Eugene 97405

Urban Farm
School of Architecture & Allied Arts
University of Oregon
Eugene 97403

Organically Grown Cooperative
1640 Beacon Drive
Eugene 97404

BRING (Being Recycled in Natural Groups)
Box 885
Eugene 97440

Center for Environmental Action
PO Box 188
Cottage Grove 97424

Cascade Holistic Economic Consultants
EMU Suite 1
University of Oregon
Eugene 97403

Center for Environmental Research
Architecture and Allied Arts
University of Oregon
Eugene 97403

Citizens Against Toxic Sprays
1385 Bailey Avenue
Eugene 97402
344-0252, 345-6237

Environmental Studies Center
University of Oregon
Eugene 97403
686-5006

Northwest Coalition for Alternatives to Pesticides
Box 375
Eugene 97440
344-5044

Oregon Wilderness Coalition
PO Box 3066
Eugene 97403
686-5014

Oregonians Cooperating to Protect Whales
873 Willamette
Eugene 97401

Second Growth
1050 W. 3rd
Eugene 97402
485-5502

Evergreen Recycling
48277 First Street
Oakridge 97463

Garbagio's, Inc.
Box 1843
Eugene 97440
485-4209

Survival Center
EMU. Suite 1
University of Oregon
Eugene 97403

Synergistic Ecological Action
873 Willamette
Eugene 97401
485=5145

Hoedad's Co-op, Inc.
PO Box 10107
Eugene 97440
485-2424

Land, Air, and Water
School of Law
University of Oregon
Eugene 97403

Marcola Recycling Center
94590 Johnson Road
Marcola 97454
933-2406

McKenzie Guardians
51013 McKenzie Highway
Finn Rock 97401
822-3379

McKenzie River Co-op
Huckleberry Lane
Finn Rock 97401

North Umpqua Preservation Association
Box 732
Cottage Grove, Oregon 97424

Trojan Decommissioning Alliance
348 West 8th
Eugene 97401

Willamette Community Design Center
1795½ Agate
Box 10273
Eugene 97440
345-2427

Willamette River Chautaqua
2157 Patterson #4
Eugene 97405

Willamette River Greenway Association
2006 Grant
Eugene 97405

* *

Health and Children

The following organizations provide the community with low cost health care, health education, and other services, such as aid with natural or home birth, which are not traditionally provided by the American health care industry.

Birthright
795 Willamette
Eugene 97401
485-8021

Centre for Wholistic Birth
1923 E. 19th
Eugene 97405
484-4853

Community Health and Education Center
433 W. 10th
Eugene 97402
485-8445 (office)
485-5782 (medical)

Community Mental Health Consultants
1857 University
Eugene 97403
342-5717

Drug Information Center
1763 Moss
Eugene 97403
686-5411

Eugene Hearing and Speech Center
1202 Almaden
Box 2087
Eugene 97402
485-8521

Great Oaks School of Health
82644 N. Howe Lane
Creswell 97426
895-4967, 895-2440

HOME of Eugene
(Home Oriented Maternity Experience)
645 E. 31st
Eugene 97405
686-8209

Lane County ASPO-La Maze Prepared Childbirth
Box 5083
Eugene 97405
689-3482

Lane Group Health Services
1400 High
Eugene 97401
485-1850

McKenzie River Clinic
Box 183
Blue River 97413
822-3341

LaLeche League
598 Park
Eugene 97404
688-7583

Mental Health for Children
3995 Marcola Road
Springfield 97477
726-1465

Planned Parenthood Association of Lane County
134 East 13th, Suite E
Eugene 97401
344-1611, 344-9411

Right to Life
1849 Willamette, #10
Eugene 97401
485-4747

Teen Clinic
134 East 13th
Eugene 97402
344-9411, 344-1611

White Bird Sociomedical Aid Station
341 East 12th
Eugene 97401
342-8255

Zero Population Growth
Box 5495
Eugene 97405

* *

Politics and Law

If fighting for legal and social justice sounds
like an interesting way to spend your spare time,
the organizations could use your help. If you
are seeking justice for yourself, it is possible
that one or more of them could help you.

Amnesty International
1361 W. Broadway
Eugene 97402

Clergy and Laity Concerned
1414 Kincaid
Eugene 97401

Eugene Committee for a Free Chile
547½ East 13th
Eugene 97401

Lane Count American Civil Liberties Union
1236 Kincaid
Eugene 97401

Lane County Legal Aid Service
1309 Willamette
Eugene 97401

League of Women Voters
1240 West 15th
Eugene 97402

National Lawyers Guild
School of Law, Room 115
University of Oregon
Eugene 97403

New American Movement
Box 3120
Eugene 97403

Oregon Student Public Interest Research Group
EMU Suite 1
University of Oregon
Eugene, Oregon 97403

People's Law School
School of Law
University of Oregon
Eugene 97403

Senior Law Service
1309 Willamette
Eugene 97401

Women's Law Forum
School of Law
University of Oregon
Eugene 97403

Arts and Crafts Organizations

If you're an artist it will be profitable for you to know about these Lane County groups.

Arts Alliance, Lane County
Box 1906
Eugene 97401

Community Art Studio
37 N. Madison
Eugene 97401

Community Center for the Performing Arts
291 West 8th
Eugene 97402

Lane Regional Arts Council
795 Willamette, #409
Eugene 97401

Mastercraft Cooperative
2041 Main Street
Springfield 97477

New Mime Circus
343 High
Eugene 97401

Open Gallery
497 High
Eugene 97401

Re-Create
301 N. Adams
Eugene 97402

Saturday Market
Box 427
Eugene 97440

Sew-Op
233 Bogart
Eugene 97401

Northwest Artisan's Network
1553½ Charnelton
Eugene 97401
343-2403

Oz Publications
Box 124
Eugene 97440
343-3496

White Light Media Arts
516 Madison
Eugene 97402

Oregon Volunteer Lawyers for the Arts
1291 Highway 99N
Eugene 97402

•••

Education

The following organizations provide a multi-tude of educational services outside the regular public school program in Eugene. Their services range from regular school programs to day care, from religious education to vocational education, from marriage education to educational services for the handicapped.

Birth to Three
2374 Onyx
Eugene 97403
484-4401

Community Childcare Resource Center
521 Kourt Drive
Eugene 97404
689-7718

Edcentric Magazine
454 Willamette
Box 10085
Eugene 97440
343-0810

Lane County 4-C Council
751½ West 7th
Eugene 97402
342-5456

Literacy Council of Eugene-Springfield
49 E. 11th
Eugene 97401
344-0051

Mohawk Valley Learning Center
Box 660
Marcola 97454
933-2882, 933-2581

Human Life Center
1849 Willamette, #10
Eugene 97401
485-4747

Eugene Montessori School
2255 Oakmont Way
Eugene, Oregon 97401
345-7124

Oregon Upward Trend
Box 5152
Eugene 97405
485-6956

Eugene Bible College
2155 Bailey Hill Road
Eugene, Oregon 97405
485-1780

Saint Alice School
1510 F. Street
Springfield 97477
746-5213

Union Point School
2795 Monroe
Eugene 97405
485-3670

Marriage Education Center
Box 5414
Eugene 97405
342-1010

Eugene Business College, Inc.
383 E. 11th
Eugene 97401
345-3413

Community Childcare Resource Center
751½ West 7th
Eugene 97402
344-5660

Good Shepherd Day Care Center
32 Marion Lane
Eugene 97404
688-8941

Educational Environments School
5510 Fox Hollow Road
Eugene 97405
345-1216

Eugene Seed Center Preschool
1515 River Loop #1
Eugene 97404
689-7566, 343-2432

Eugene Waldorf School Association
Covenant Presbyterian Church
3800 Ferry
Eugene 97405
686-8209

Institute for Human Beginnings
140 E. 39th
Eugene 97405
343-4825

Pearl Buck Center
5100 W. Amazon Drive
Eugene 97405
345-8506

The Easter Seal School and Treatment Center
3575 Donald
Eugene 97405
344-2247

Northwest Christian College
11th & Alder
Eugene 97401
343-1641

Marist High School
1900 Kingsley Road
Eugene 97401
686-5351

Preschool for Multiply Handicapped
University of Oregon
Center on Human Development
Clinical Services Building
Eugene, 97403

Eugene Christian School
4500 W. Amazon
Eugene 97405
686-9145, 485-1791

O'Hara Catholic School
715 W. 18th Avenue
Eugene 97402
345-1045

● ●

Economic Aid

The following organizations offer economic aid to the people of Eugene. The aid, depending on the organization, may be a loan or a grant of money, tools, or labor, or it may take the form of information or research, or it may be the teaching of some money-management skill.

Community Energy Bank
454 Willamette
Eugene 97401
484-8133

Labor, Education & Research Center
154 PLC
University of Oregon
Eugene 97403
686-5054

Lane Economic Development Council
Box 1473
Eugene 97440
484-7007

OUR Credit Union
795 Willamette, #206
Eugene 97401
485-1188

Pacific Northwest Research Center
Box 3708
Eugene 97403
686-5125

Tool Library
1557 Agate
Eugene 97403
686-3702

Upper Willamette Economic Development
    Corporation
Box 956
Oakridge 97463
782-3742

●●●

Humanities

Information, referral, advocacy, counseling. Chances are that if you have a question, a problem, or a cause, one of the following organizations will be able to help you.

Cascadian Regional Library
454 Willamette
Box 1492
Eugene 97440
485-0366   231

Switchboard
454 Willamette
Eugene 97401
686-8453

Displaced Homemakers-Widowed Services
1609 Agate
Eugene 97403
686-4220

Eugene Emergency Housing
(Family Shelter House)
 367 Highway 99N
Eugene 97402
689-7156

Eugene Senior Lobby
1130 W. 25th
Eugene 97405
343-9870

Family Counseling Services of Lane County
1432 Orchard
Eugene 97403
485-5111

Gray Panthers
Celeste Campbell Senior Center
155 High
Eugene 97401
688-3975, 687-9519

Lane Interagency Network
1134 Ferry
Eugene 97401
342-4451

Hands Across the Walls
Box 10583
Eugene 97440

Lane County Open Door for Adoptable Children
St. Mary's Episcopal Church
13th & Pearl
Eugene 97401
343-8753

Looking Glass Family Crisis Intervention Center
795 Willamette, #410
Eugene 97401
686-2688 (Administration)
689-3111 (Crisis)

Parents Anonymous
2502 Jeppeson Acres
Eugene 97401
687-4000

Rape Crisis Network
Box 5152
Eugene 97405
485-6700

Lane County Direction Service
1736½ Moss Street
Eugene, 97403
686-3598

Exceptional Family Advocacy
Center on Human Development
University of Oregon
Eugene 97403

Sponsors, Inc.
690 Tyler
Eugene 97402
485-8341

Springfield Voluntary Action Center
765 N. A
Springfield 97477

Voluntary Action Center
1134 Ferry
Eugene 97401
342-4451

●●●

CARES

Client Assistance, Referral,
and Evaluation System (CARES)

CARES deserves special mention in this
section. This is the most comprehensive information and referral service in Eugene. They
have information on all public and private
agencies, skilled listeners who may be able
to help you solve your problems, emergency mental
health aid, and information on health and social
services available to all people in Eugene.
CARES is open 24 hours, every day.

CARES
170 E. 11th
Eugene 97401
687-4000
1-800- 452-7041 (toll free)

• •

Senior Services

The following organizations provide services
for senior citizens.

Trude Kaufman Senior Center
996 Jefferson Street
687-5331

Sorgenfri Nutrition Site
3400 Hawthorne Street
689-3483

Bethel Danebo Nutrition Site
3400 Hawthorne Street
689-8011

234

First Christian Church Nutrition Site
1166 Oak Street
344-1425

Maxi Taxi
Lane County Senior Services
687-4083

Senior Information Coordinator
Delayne Will
Eugene Parks and Recreation District
City Hall II
858 Pearl Street
687-5333

Index

236

Villard Hall 15,46
Villard, Henry 15-16
Vincent, Andrew 54

W

Walden 171
Ward, Jean Camille 52
Warner, Gertrude Bass 55
Washburne, Carl G., State
    Park 88
Washburne Park 14
Washington Hand Press 45
Watts House 22
Watts, J. O. 22
Weather 190-194
Western Exchange 171
West Sixth Motel 178
White, Dr. Elijah 20
Whiteaker, John 5,12,30
Wild Iris Pottery 156
Wildlife in Oregon 200
Wild Plum Restaurant 113
Willamette High School 60
Willamette Meteorite 42
Willamette National Forest 75
Willamette Oracle Group 53
Willamette Pass 99
Willamette People's Co-op
    163
Willamette Science and
    Technology Center 66
Willamette Valley Observer 59
William L. Finley National
    Wildlife Refuge 95
Williams Bakery Thrift
    Stores 167
Winchester, Oregon 4
Winchester Bay fishing
    Information 74
Wind 191
Woodstoves 199

Woolworth's Harvest House
    Restaurant 124
Worldly Goods Sales
    Service 161
WOW Hall 63

Y

Yachats, Oregon 90
YMCA 77

Z

Zach, Jan 48,51,52,53
Zybach's Delicatessen
    103

Notes